ESTATE PUBLICATIONS

CUMBRIA

Street maps with index
Administrative Districts
Road Map with index
Postcodes

COUNTY RED BOOKS

This atlas is intended for those requiring street maps of the historical and commercial centres of towns within the county.   Each locality is normally presented on one or two pages and although, with many small towns, this space is sufficient to portray the whole urban area, the maps of large towns and cities are for centres only and are not intended to be comprehensive.   Such coverage in Super and Local Red Books (see page 2).

Every effort has been made to verify the accuracy of information in this book but the publishers cannot accept responsibility for expense or loss caused by any error or omission. Information that will be of assistance to the user of these maps will be welcomed.

The representation of a road, track or footpath on the maps in this atlas is no evidence of the existence of a right of way.

Street plans prepared and published by ESTATE PUBLICATIONS, Bridewell House, TENTERDEN, KENT.
The Publishers acknowledge the co-operation of the local authorities
of towns represented in this atlas.

Ordnance Survey®

This product includes mapping data licensed from Ordnance Survey®
with the permission of the Controller of Her Majesty's Stationery Office.

COUNTY RED BOOK

CUMBRIA

contains street maps for each town centre

SUPER & LOCAL RED BOOKS

are street atlases with comprehensive local coverage

CARLISLE & PENRITH

including: Brampton, Dalston, Gretna, Houghton,
Longtown, Scotby, Wetheral, Wigton etc.

KENDAL & WINDERMERE

including: Ambleside, Bowness-on-Windermere, Burneside,
Grasmere, Oxenholme, Staveley, Storrs, Troutbeck Bridge etc.

WORKINGTON & WHITEHAVEN

including: Cleator Moor, Cockermouth, Distington,
Egremont, Flimby, Gosforth, Great Broughton,
Maryport, Seaton, Sellafield etc.

CONTENTS

LEGEND TO STREET MAPS

One-Way Street	→	Post Office	●
Pedestrianized	▨	Public Convenience	C
Car Park	P	Place of Worship	+

Scale of street plans: 4 Inches to 1 mile (unless otherwise stated on the map).

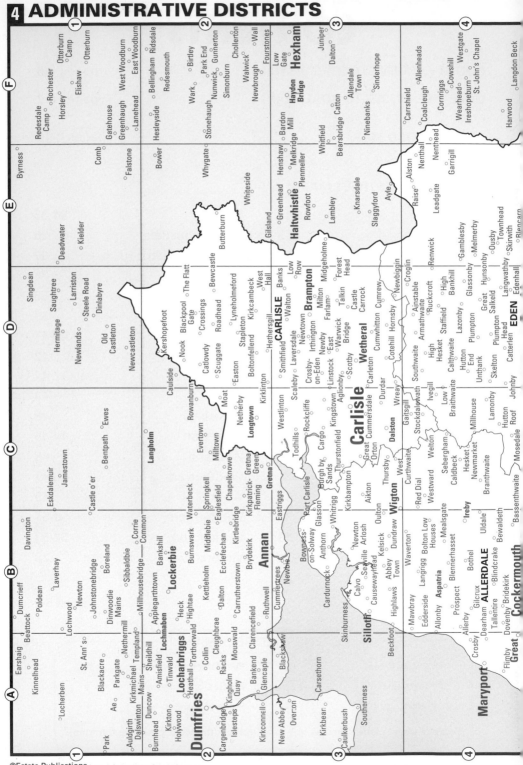

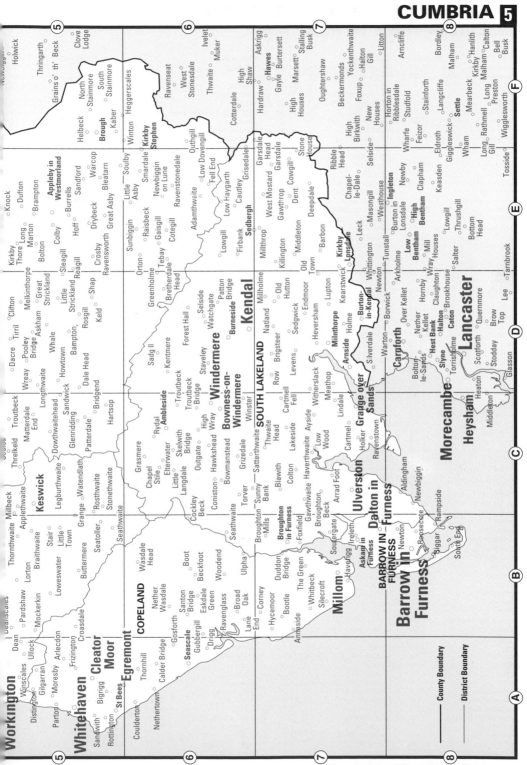

GAZETTEER INDEX TO ROAD MAP

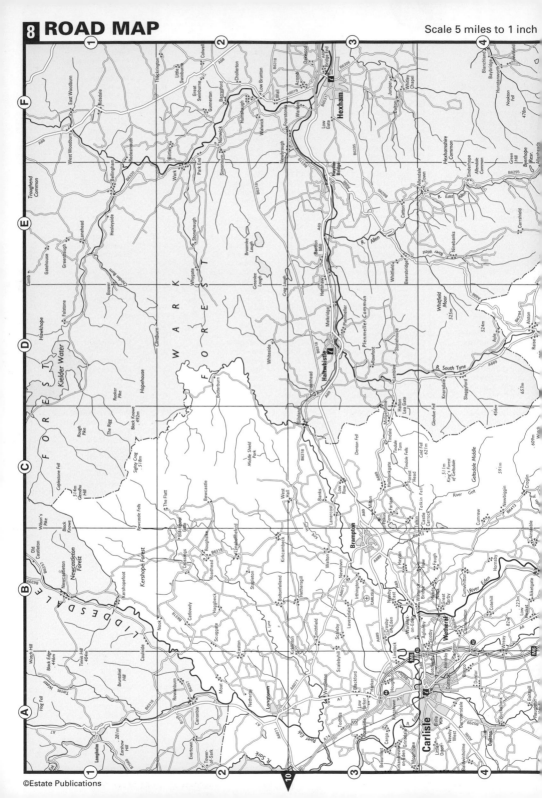

©Estate Publications

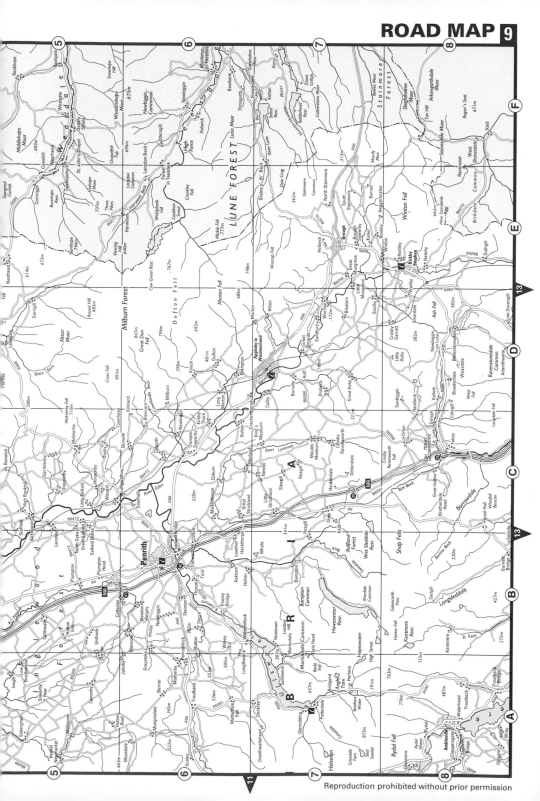

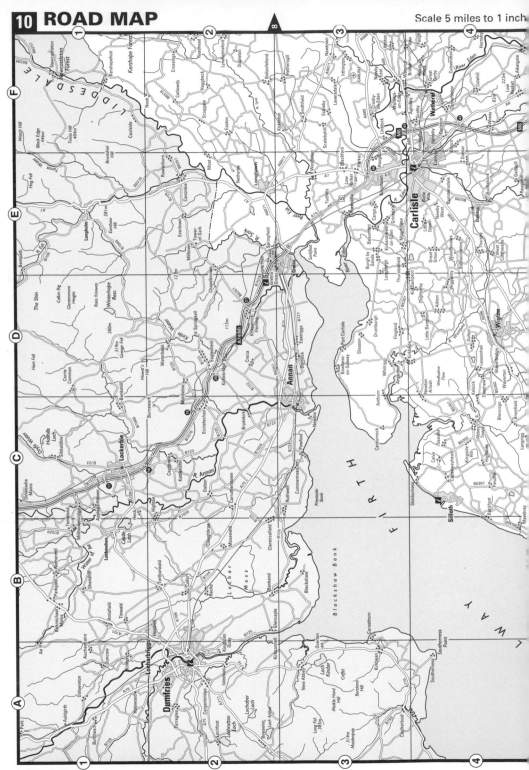

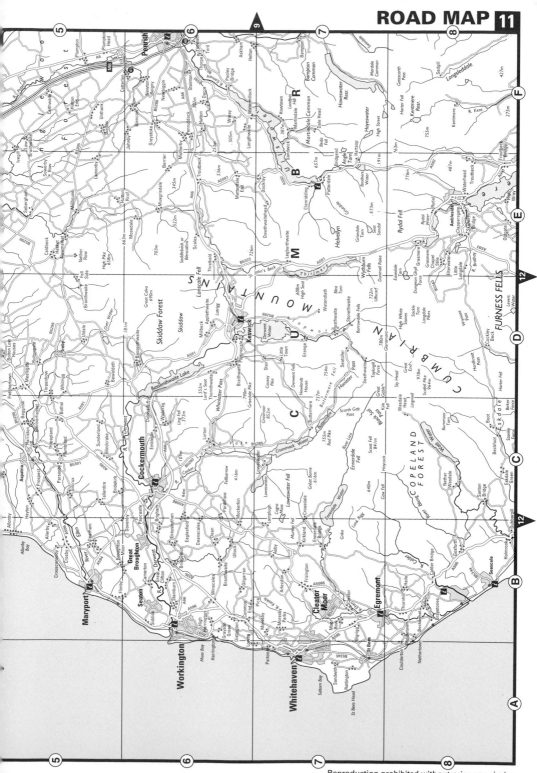

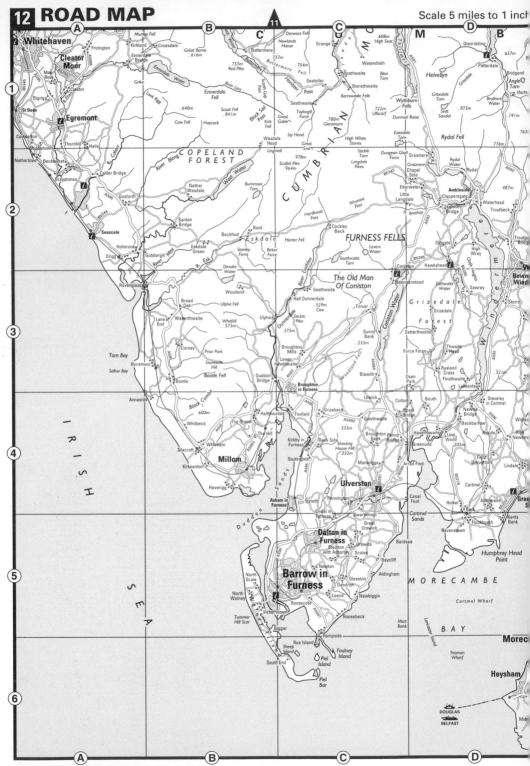

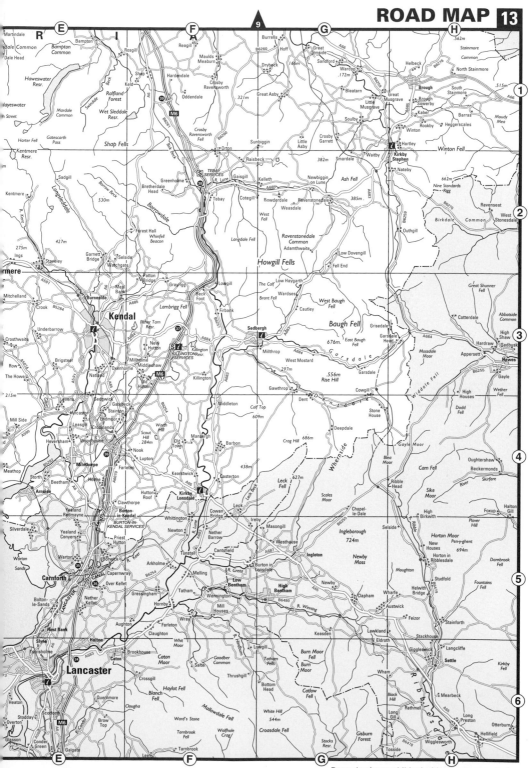

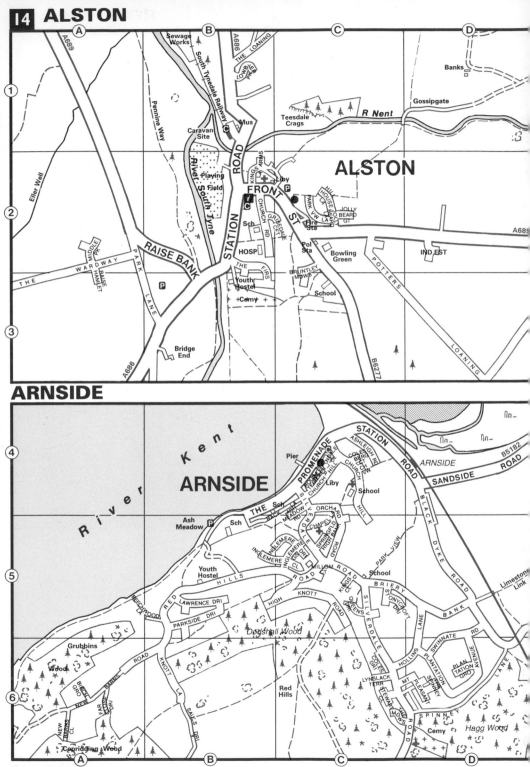

ARNSIDE

©Estate Publications

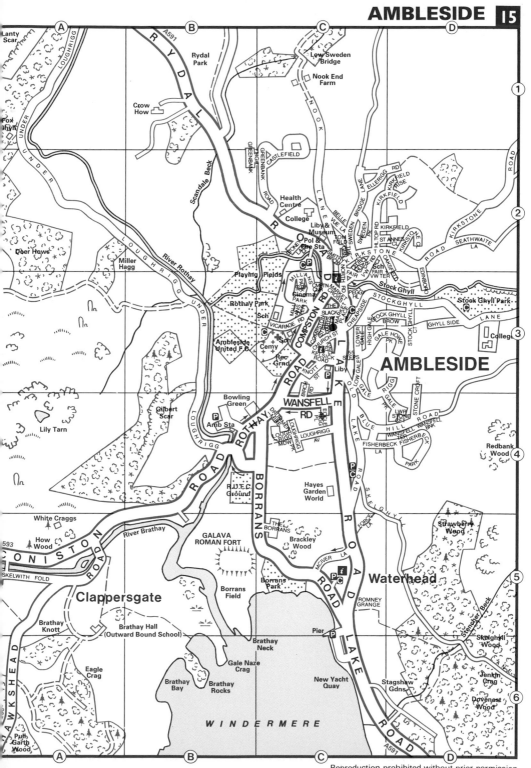

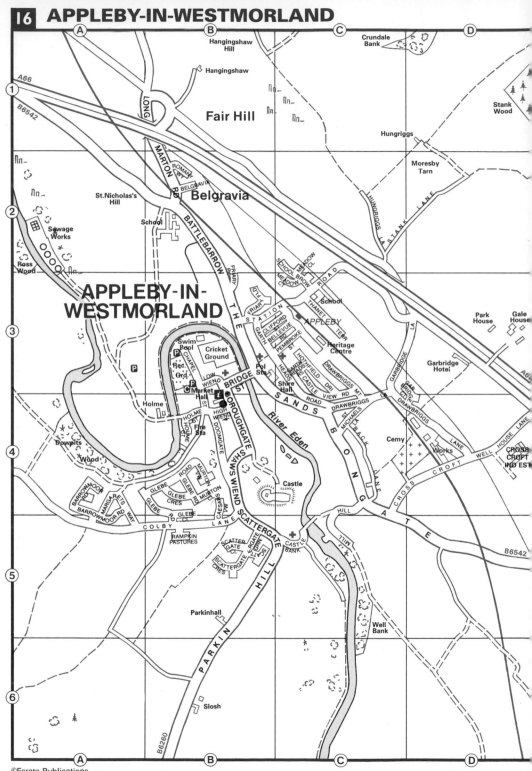

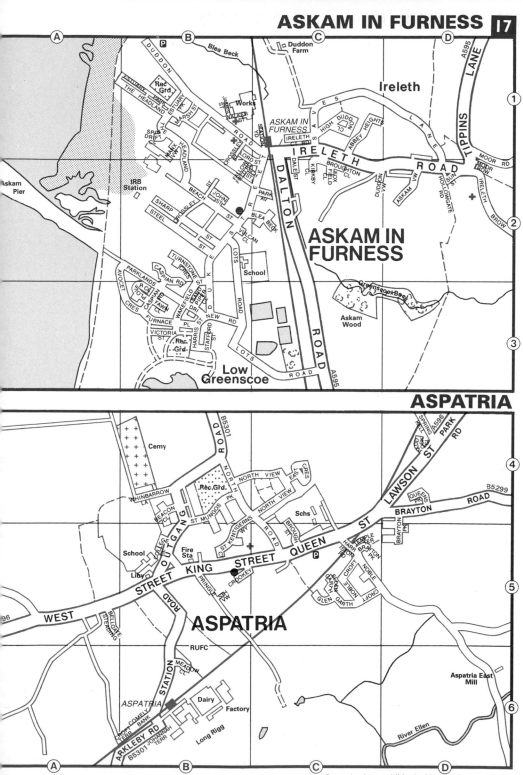

ASKAM IN FURNESS

ASPATRIA

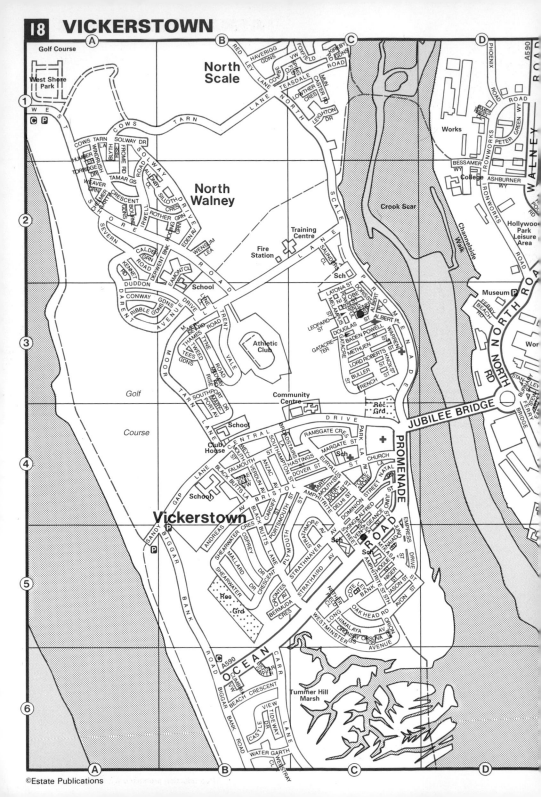

North Scale

North Walney

Golf Course

West Shore Park

Training Centre

Fire Station

Athletic Club

Community Centre

Club House

Vickerstown

Golf

Course

Crook Scar

Hollywood Park Leisure Area

Channelside Walk

Museum

JUBILEE BRIDGE

PROMENADE

Tummer Hill Marsh

Works

College

Bessemer Wy

Ashburner Wy

Ironworks

North Road

Walney

©Estate Publications

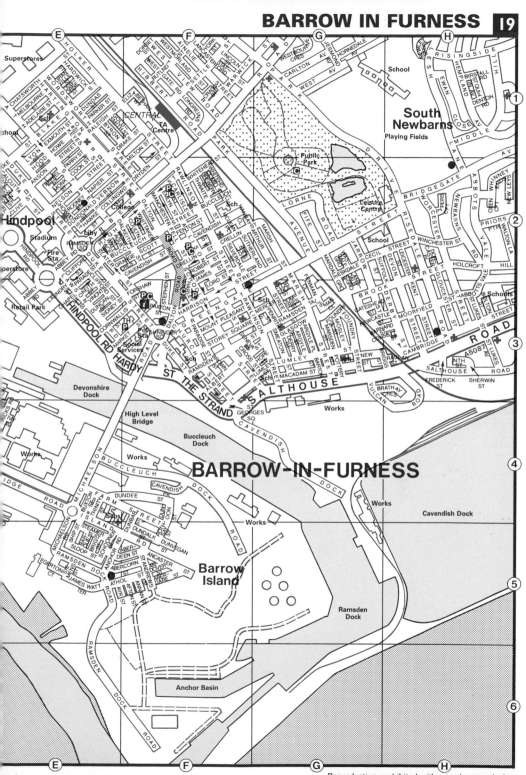

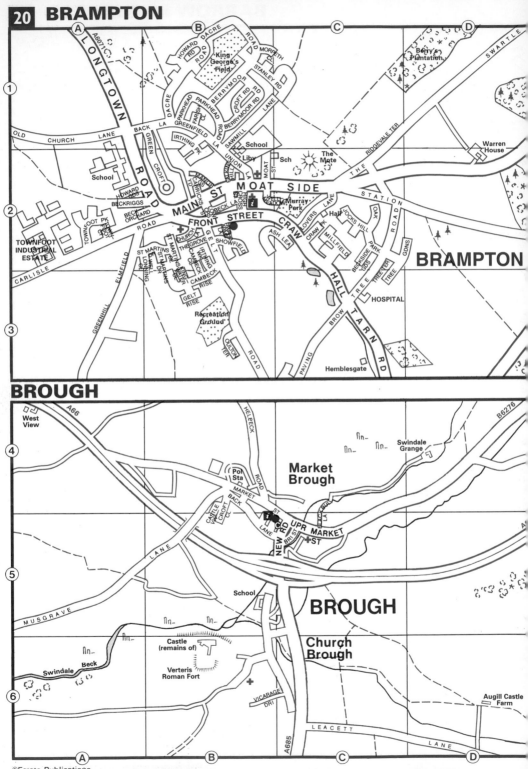

A   B   C   D

1

BRAMPTON

LONGTOWN ROAD
A6071
HOWARD RD
DACRE ROAD
MORPETH CL
SWARTLE
Berry's Plantation
King George's Field
STANLEY RD
PARKHEAD
PARKFIELD
CROFT RD
FARIS
BERRYMOOR RD
SAWMILL
BERRYMOOR RD
GREENFIELD LA
IRTHING PK
DACRE LA
BACK GREEN
CROFT
MANOR ST
UNION LANE
School
Liby
Sch
MOAT ST
The Mote
Warren House
THE RIDGEVALE TER

OLD CHURCH LANE

2

School
HOWARD RD
BECKRIGGS
BECK ORCHARD
TOWNFOOT PK
MAIN ST
CARRICKS LA
CROSS
GOOSEBECK LA
MOAT SIDE
SAXON
Murray Park
STATION
OAK TREE
GDNS
MADOX HILL
LOVERS LANE
FRONT STREET
CAROLL
CRAW
ASH LEA
SHOWFIELD
CAMBECK
IRTHING
THE GROVE
ST MARTINS DR
ST MARTINS
ST MARTINS
LOWTHER
GELT
CAMBECK
CAMBECK RISE
GELT RISE
BESKSIDE GDNS
PARK
TREE TER
TREE TER
TREE
MILLFIELD
CRAW BROW
OULTON TER
CARLISLE
GREENHILL
ELMFIELD
Recreation Ground
HALL TARN RD
HOSPITAL

BRAMPTON

3

ROAD
PAVING BROW
Hemblesgate

BROUGH

A   B   C   D

West View
A66
HELBECK ROAD
B6276
Swindale Grange

4

Market Brough
Pol Sta
MARKET
BACK
LANE
NEW RD
UPR MARKET
ST
BLACK BULL LA
CASTLE
CASTLE CROFT
BRIST

5

MUSGRAVE
LANE

BROUGH

School
Swindale Beck
Castle (remains of)
Verteris Roman Fort
Church Brough

6

VICARAGE DRI
Augill Castle Farm
A685
LEACETT LANE

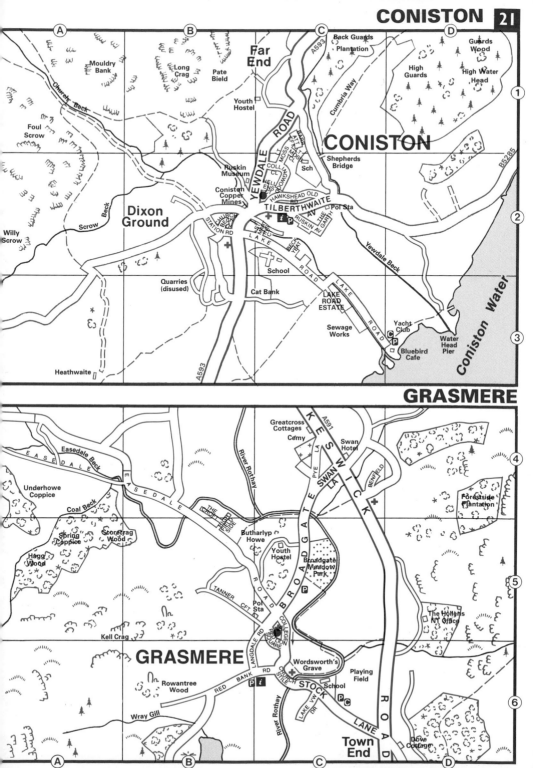

CONISTON

- Mouldry Bank
- Long Crag
- Pate Bield
- Far End
- Back Guards Plantation
- Guards Wood
- High Guards
- High Water Head
- Church Beck
- Youth Hostel
- Cumbria Way
- Foul Scrow
- YEWDALE ROAD
- Ruskin Museum
- Coniston Copper Mines
- Shepherds Bridge
- Sch
- COLL
- B5285
- Willy Scrow
- Scrow
- Beck
- Dixon Ground
- STATION RD
- TILBERTHWAITE
- HAWKSHEAD OLD RD
- Pol Sta
- RUSKIN AV
- Yewdale Beck
- School
- Quarries (disused)
- Cat Bank
- LAKE ROAD ESTATE
- Sewage Works
- Yacht Club
- Water Head Pier
- Bluebird Cafe
- Coniston Water
- Heathwaite
- A593

GRASMERE

- Easedale Beck
- Greatcross Cottages
- Cemy
- Swan Hotel
- KESWICK
- A591
- SWAN LA
- PYE LA
- BENFIELD
- Underhowe Coppice
- EASEDALE ROAD
- River Rothay
- Forestside Plantation
- Coal Beck
- THE CROFT
- Spring Coppice
- Scorecrag Wood
- Butharlyp Howe
- BROADGATE
- Hagg Wood
- Youth Hostel
- Broadgate Meadow Park
- The Hollens NT Office
- TANNER CFT
- Pol Sta
- COLLEGE
- RED BANK ROAD
- Kell Crag
- LANGDALE RD
- **GRASMERE**
- COLLEGE SQUARE
- Wordsworth's Grave
- Playing Field
- Rowantree Wood
- STOCK LANE
- LAKE VW DR
- School
- CHURCH STILE
- Wray Gill
- River Rothay
- **Town End**
- Dove Cottage

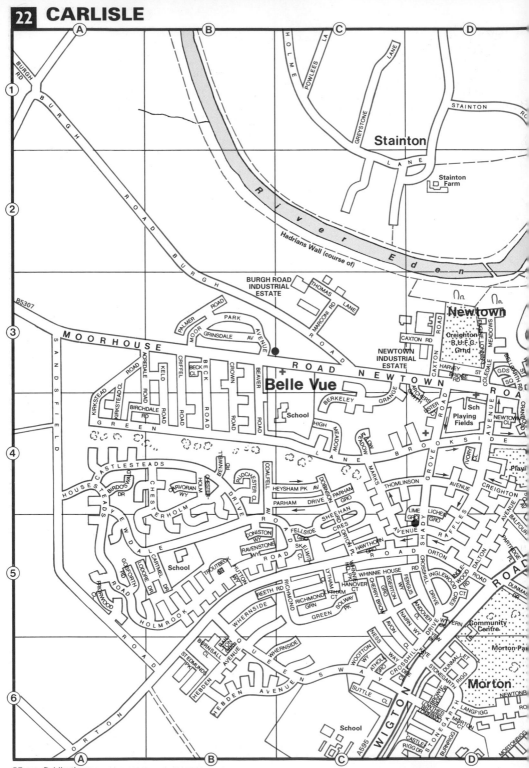

Stainton

Stainton Farm

Newtown

Creighton B.U.F.C. Grnd

NEWTOWN INDUSTRIAL ESTATE

BURGH ROAD INDUSTRIAL ESTATE

BURGH RD

BURGH ROAD

B5307

MOORHOUSE

River Eden

Hadrians Wall (course of)

Belle Vue

School

Morton

Morton Pk

Community Centre

WIGTON

A595

School

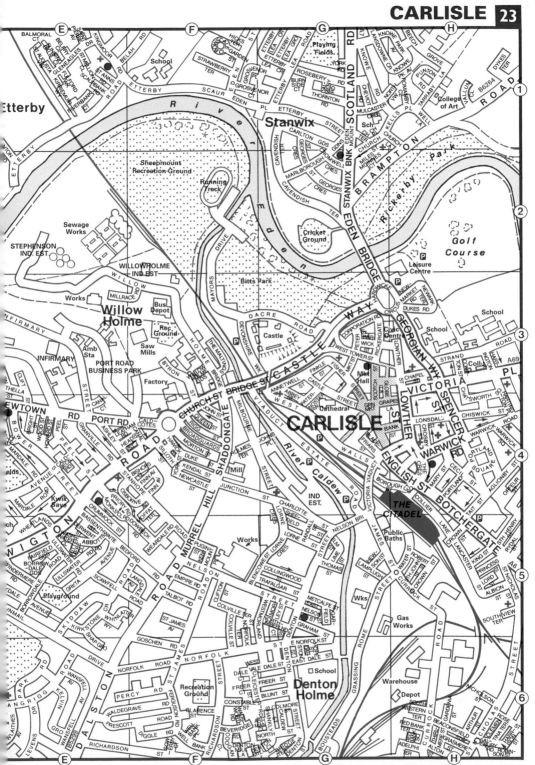

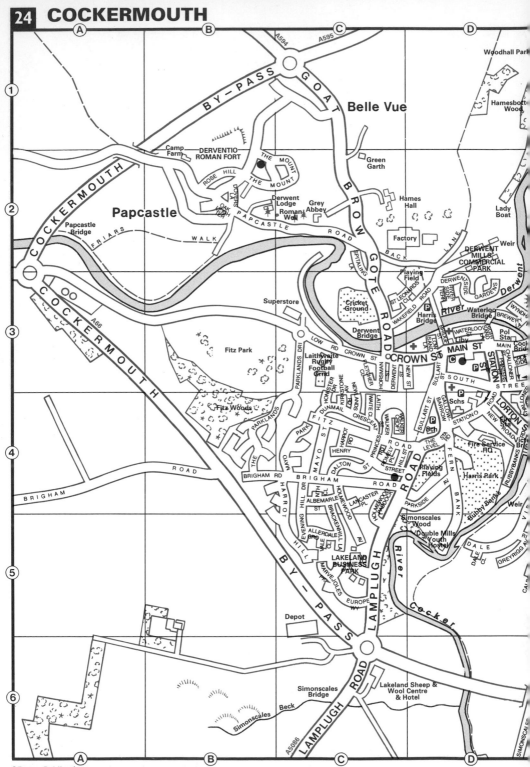

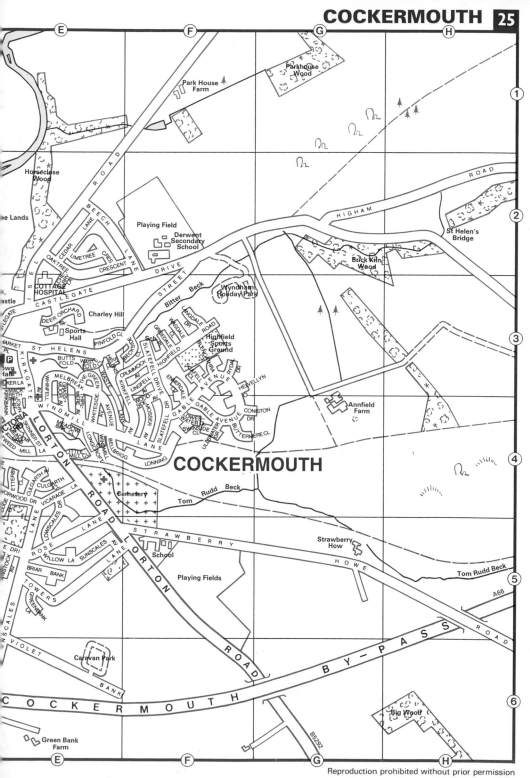

COCKERMOUTH

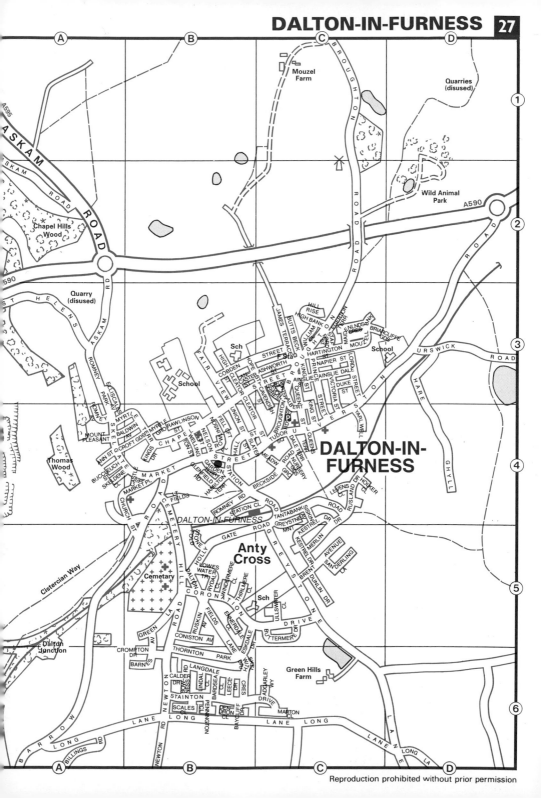

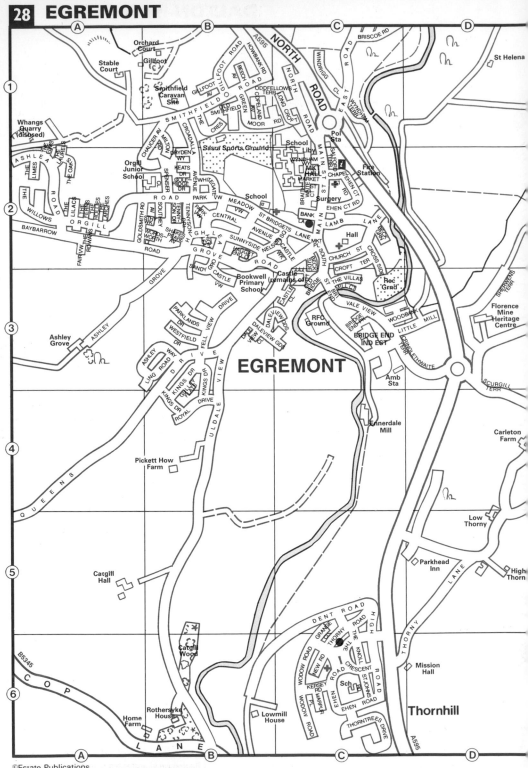

EGREMONT

Thornhill

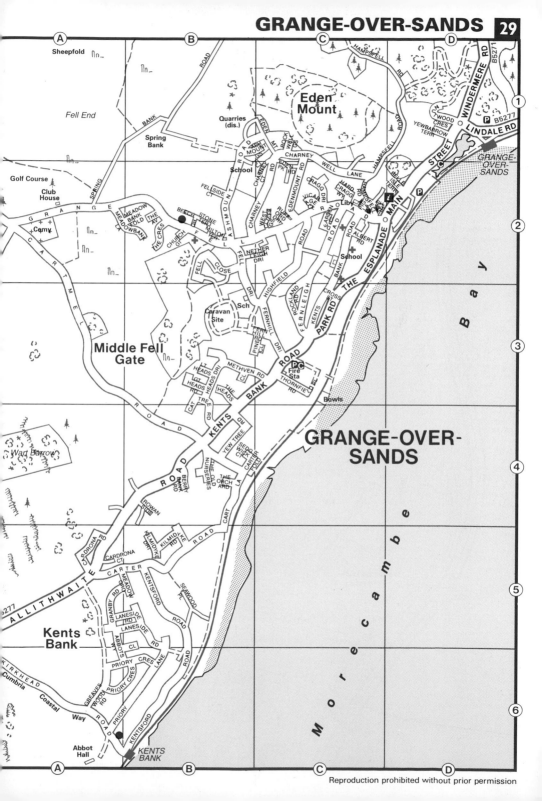

Sheepfold

Fell End

Spring Bank

Golf Course
Club House
Cemy

Eden Mount

Quarries (dis.)

School

Middle Fell Gate

Wart Barrow

Kents Bank

GRANGE-OVER-SANDS

Morecambe Bay

Caravan Site

Fire Sta

Bowls

Abbot Hall

KENTS BANK

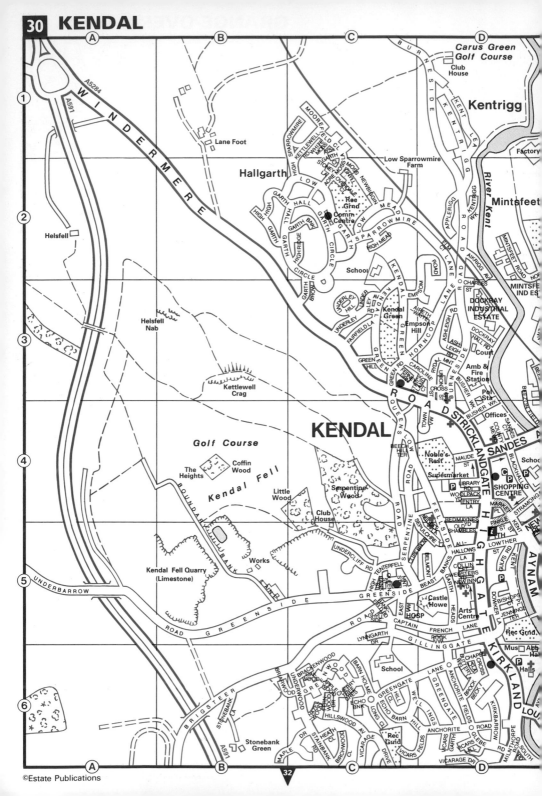

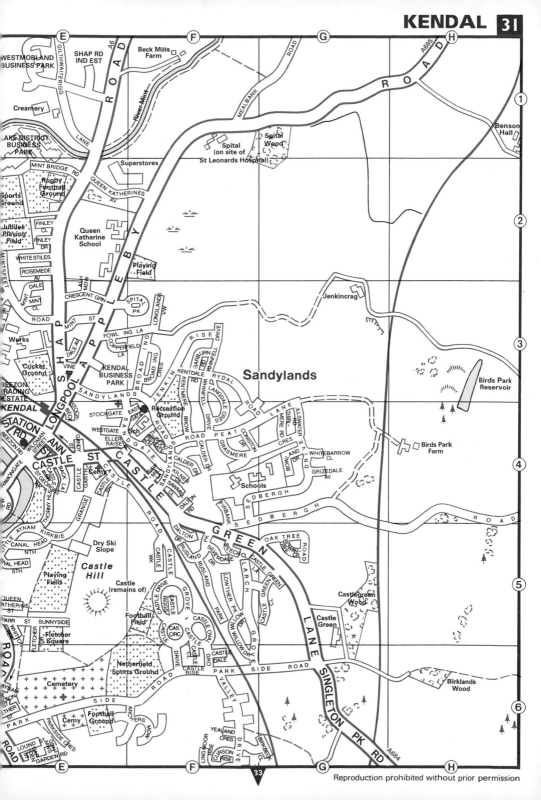

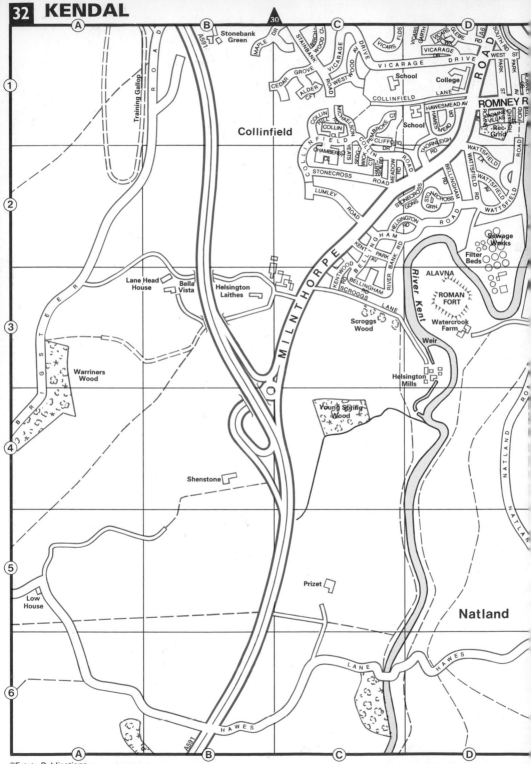

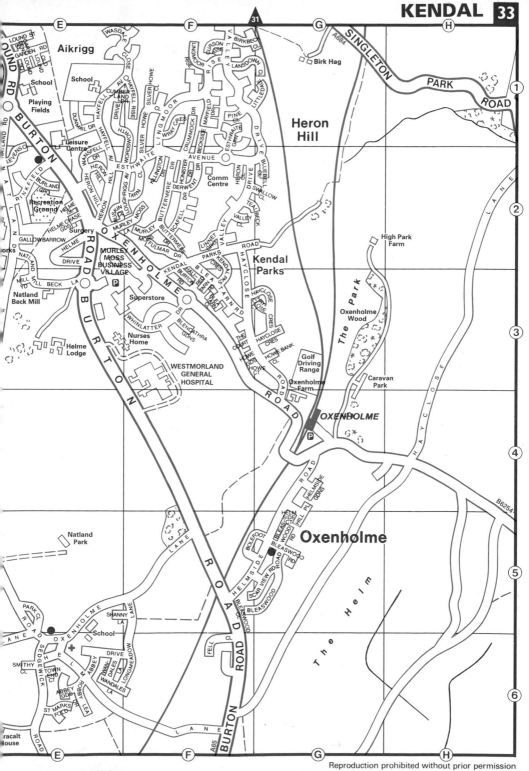

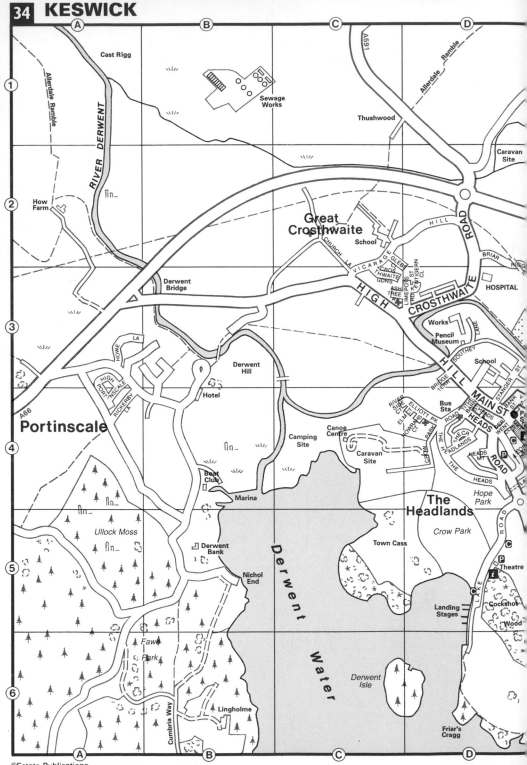

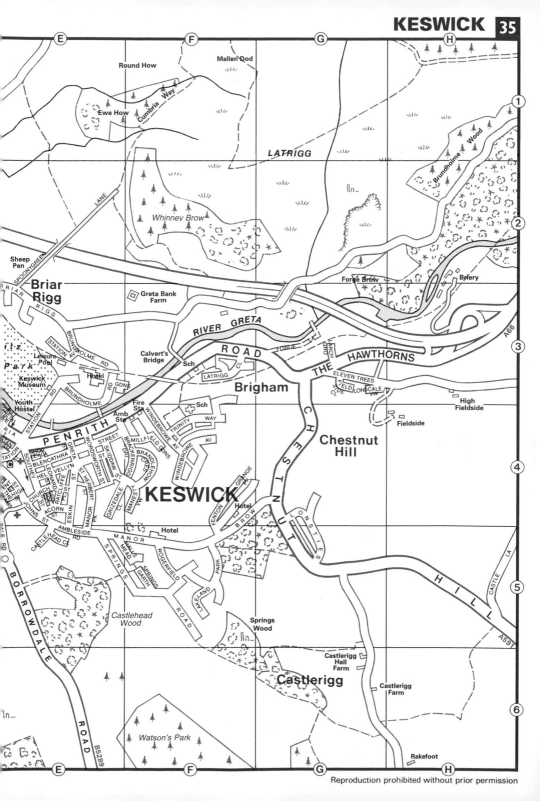

Round How
Mallen Dod
Ewe How
Cumbria Way
LANE
LATRIGG
Brundholme Wood
Whinney Brow
Sheep Pen
SPOONYGREEN
Briar Rigg
RIAR RIGG
Greta Bank Farm
Forge Brow
Briery
River Greta
A66
i l z Park
STATION AV
BRUNDHOLME RD
Leisure Pool
Calvert's Bridge
Sch
ROAD
FORGE
THE HAWTHORNS
LARCH GRO
Hotel
RD GDNS
LATRIGG CL
ELEVEN TREES FIELD LONSCALE
SIDE CL
High Fieldside
Keswick Museum
STATION RD
BRUNDHOLME RD
Fire Sta
Amb Sta
WINDEBROWE AV
Brigham
TRINITY WAY
Sch
Fieldside
Youth Hostel
CHESTNUT
Chestnut Hill
C
PENRITH STREET
WORDSWORTH ST
SKIDDAW ST
BRACKENRIGG
BRANDELHOW
WINDEBROWE AV
BLENCATHRA
HELVELLYN
ST HERBERT ST
MANOR CL
GRIZEDALE CL
SOUTHEY ST
GRETA ST
CHURCH ST
RATCLIFFE
ESKIN ST
ACORN ST
MANESTY VW
KESWICK
GRANGE PK
FENTON WAY
Hotel
BROW
LONSTIES
4
JOHNS ST
AMBLESIDE RD
Hotel
MANOR MEAD
ROGERFIELD
PARK
HILL
CASTLE LA
CASTLEHEAD CL
SPRINGS
SEBINGS GARTH
LAKELAND PARK
A591
BORROWDALE
Castlehead Wood
Springs Wood
5
ROAD
Castlerigg Hall Farm
Castlerigg Farm
Castlerigg
Watson's Park
Rakefoot
ROAD B5289
6

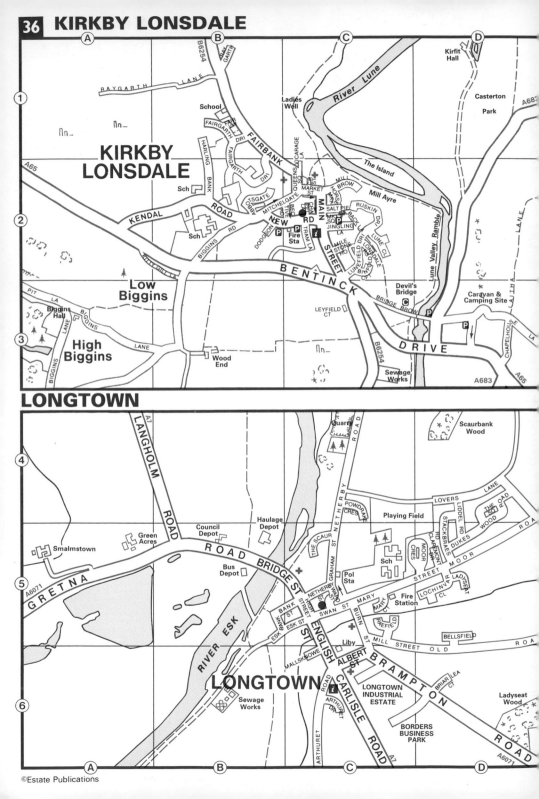

LONGTOWN

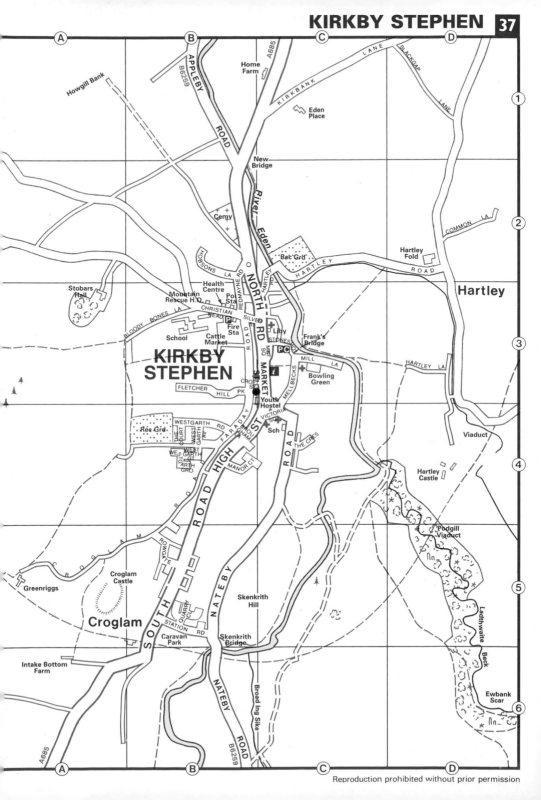

Reproduction prohibited without prior permission

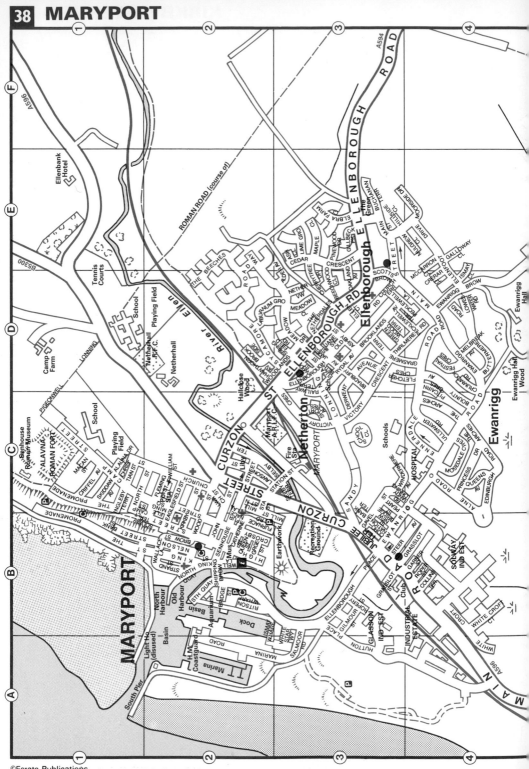

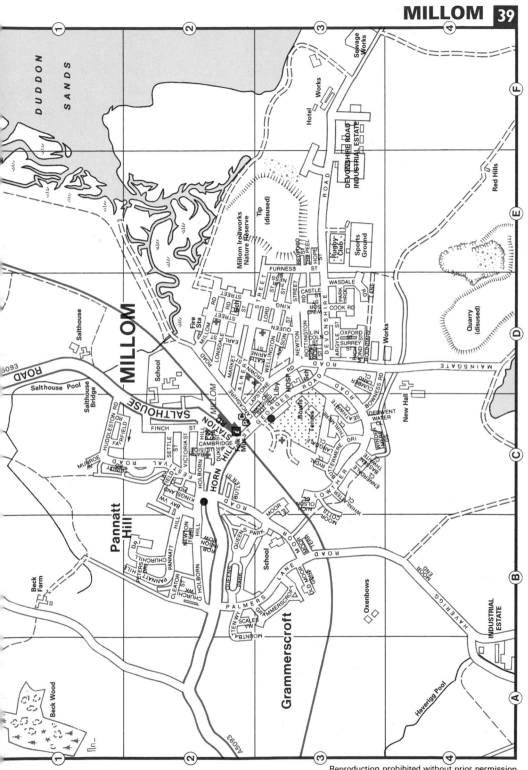

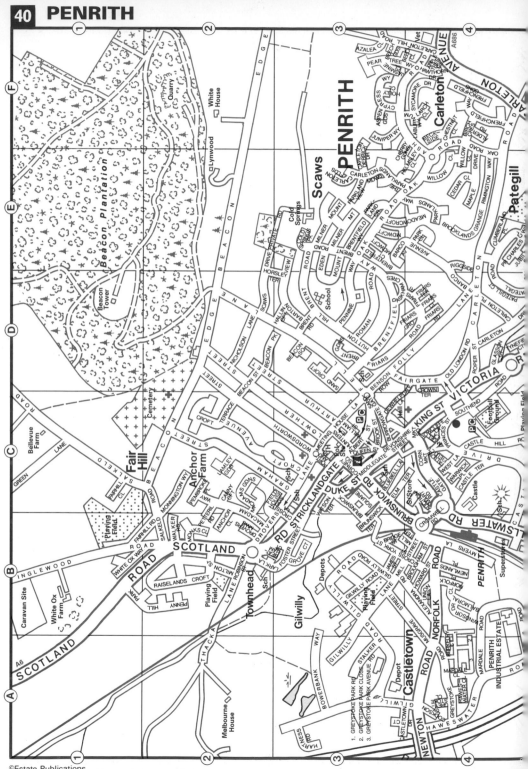

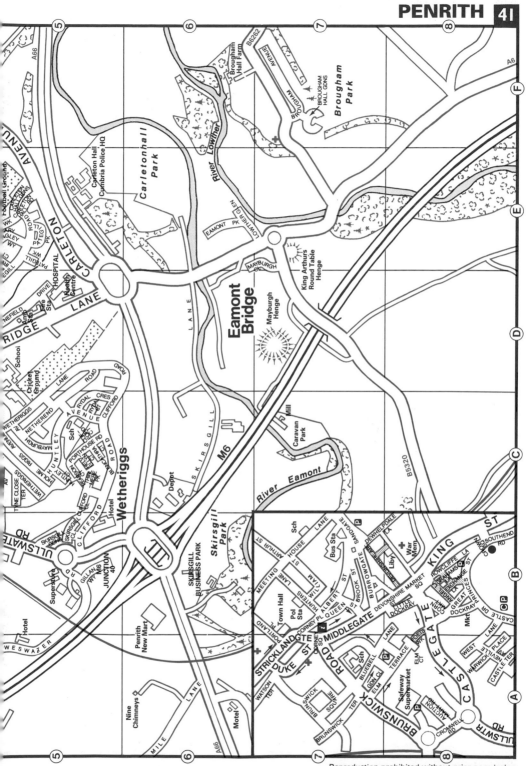

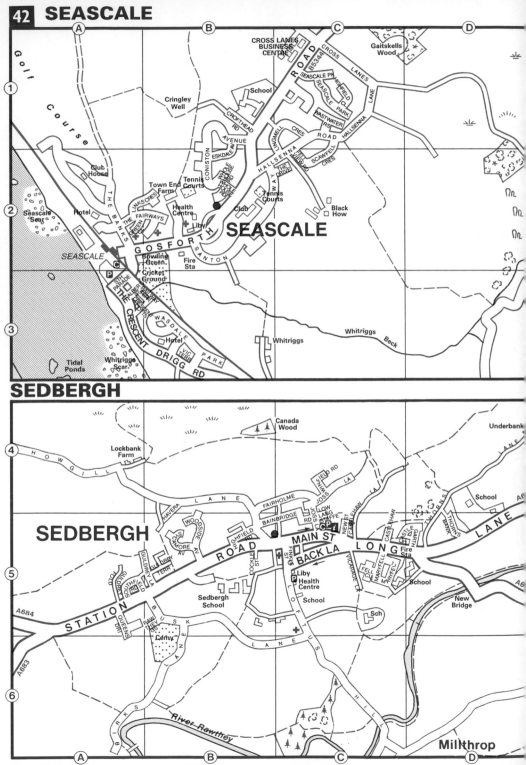

SEASCALE

Golf Course

CROSS LANES BUSINESS CENTRE

Gaitskells Wood

CROSS LANES

B5344

School

Cringley Well

SEASCALE PK

HIGHFIELD

SEASCALE PARK

LANE

WASTWATER

CROFTHEAD RD

CONISTON

AVENUE

ESKDALE

LINGMELL CRES

HALLSENNA

ROAD

HALLSENNA

SCAWFELL CRES

Club House

THE BANKS

Town End Farm

Tennis Courts

THE FAIRWAYS

LINKS CRES

THE GREEN

Health Centre

Liby

Club

Tennis Courts

THE DRIVE

Black How

SEASCALE

Hotel

Seascale Scar

SEASCALE

GOSFORTH

SANTON

P

Bowling Green

Cricket Ground

Fire Sta

THE PARADE

THE CRESCENT

THALBERG

WASDALE

Hotel

VIC TERR

PARK

DRIGG RD

Whitriggs

Whitriggs Beck

Tidal Ponds

Whitriggs Scar

SEDBERGH

Underbank

LANE

Canada Wood

Lockbank Farm

HOWGILL

MAVERA LANE

WINFIELD RD

LA

JOSS LA

FAIRHOLME

LOW LANE

JOSS LANE

NEW ST

CASTLEHAW

CASTLEHAW

School

SEDBERGH

WOODSIDE

SYCAMORE AV

HGFIELD

BAINBRIDGE

MAIN ST

STAFFE

CASTLE GARTH

THORNS BANK

LONG LANE

GULDREY TERR

STHFIELD RD

GULDREY LA

ROAD

COCKLEY ST

FINKLE ST

BACK LA

VICARAGE LA

FELL CL

MARYFELL

MARTEN

Fire Sta

THORNS

School

LANE

STATION

A684

A683

QUEENS DRI

RAWTHEY DY

BUSK LANE

Cerry

Sedbergh School

LOFTUS LANE

Liby

Health Centre

School

Sch

School

New Bridge

A6

BIRKS

River Rawthey

HILL

Millthrop

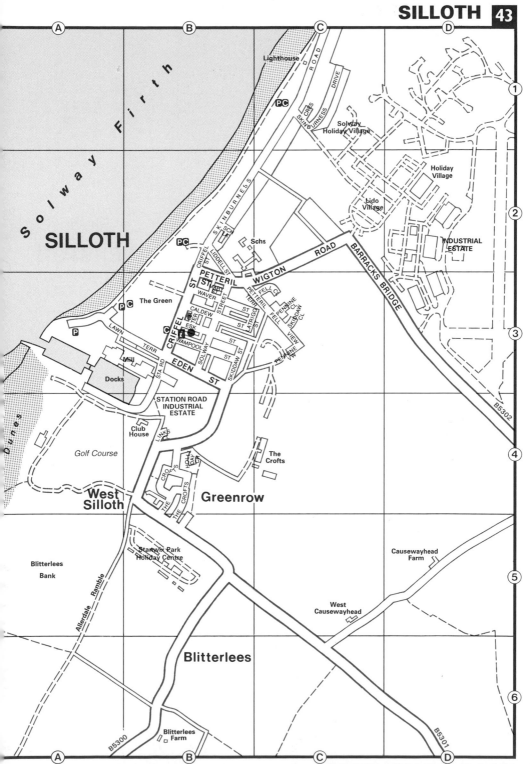

Solway Firth

Solway

SILLOTH

Dunes

Lighthouse

PC

SKINBURNESS

OLD SKINBURNESS

ROAD

DRIVE

Solway Holiday Village

Holiday Village

Lido Village

INDUSTRIAL ESTATE

Schs

PC

SKINBURNESS

WIGTON ROAD

BARRACKS BRIDGE

B5302

CRIFFEL ST
LIDDELL ST
PETTERIL ST
WAVER STREET
CALDEW
ESK
KER
WAMPOOL
SOLWAY
CRIFFEL ST
EDEN ST
STA RD
TERR
LAWN
PC
P

The Green

PETTERIL ST
FELL
PENNINE CL
SKIDDAW CL
ST
ST
LATRIGG
VIEW
PENNINE VW

ST
SKIDDAW ST

Mill

Docks

STATION ROAD INDUSTRIAL ESTATE

Club House

LINKS

Golf Course

THE CROFTS
HOLIDAY
THE CROFTS

The Crofts

West Silloth

Greenrow

Blitterlees Bank

Allerdale Ramble

Stanwix Park Holiday Centre

Causewayhead Farm

West Causewayhead

B5302

5

Blitterlees

B5300

Blitterlees Farm

B5301

6

ULVERSTON

Swarthmoor

Kilner Park

Heaning Wood

Cumbria Way

Fell Side Farm

Rosside Farm

Barn Beck

Green Moor Farm

Three Bridges

Levy Beck

Swarthmoor Hall Farm

Swarthmoor Hall

Hotel

PENNINGTON LANE

WOODLAND RD

STOCKBRIDGE LANE

TARN CL

STONECROSS GDNS

DALTON GATE

NEW CHURCH

LIGHTBURN

LIGHTBURN TRADING ESTA

ULVERSTON

MAYFIELD RD

THE DRIVE

SPRING

OLD HALL

WILLOW DENE RD

MOWINGS

HOSP

LEATHER
THE GI

FALLOWFIE
AV

RUFUS LANE

KINGSLEY AV

EAST RD

PARK RD

FOX ST

SWARTHMOOR HALL LANE

CROSS LANDS

MOORGARTH

WILLOW AV

PARK ROAD

Rec Grd

Sch

Hall

CROSS A MOOR

SOG LANE

ULVERSTON ROAD

THE LAURELS

FELL VIEW

BRACKEN GRO

HEATHER PARK

TRINKELD AV

SPRING VALE

BROOK VALE

MEADOW SIDE

FIELD PARK

BIRK RIGG

PARK SIDE

Trinkeld Farm

A590

Cistercian Way

QUAKER FOLD

CARAWAY

MEETING HOUSE LA

RUSLAND CRESCENT

WESTON

JEFFERSON DRIVE

CRESCENT

BIRKETT DRIVE

DORCHESTER CRES

CARLTON GDNS

WEST HILLS

SAVOY

WINDSOR CRES DRIVE

COLT HO

CURWICK ROAD

The Nook Farm

Driving Range

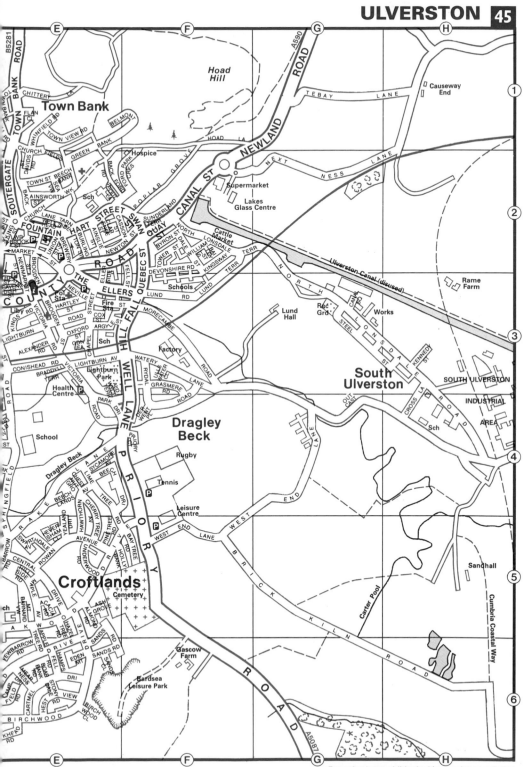

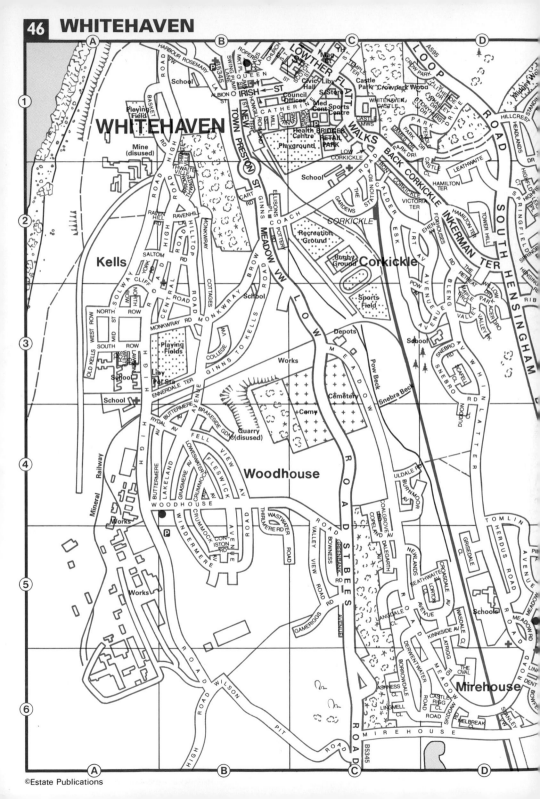

WHITEHAVEN

Kells

Corkickle

Woodhouse

Mirehouse

Standing Stones

Playing 'Field'

Moss Wood

Priestgill Wood

New Monkwray

St Benedicts RC Secondary School

Training Centre

School

Alma Bank Wood

School

Factory

RFC Ground

Whitehaven Grammar School

Overend School

Fire Sta

Cemy

Factories

School

Hensingham

Sports Grnd

Library

Overend

Ullswater Av

Martin Dale Cl

Ullswater Av

CLEATOR

Swimming Pool

Overend Quarry (disused)

GLENRIDDING

Copeland Athletics Stadium

SNECKYEAT ROAD IND EST

Warehouse

Keekle

WEST CUMBERLAND HOSPITAL

GALEMIRE

Summergrove Conference Centre

Millhill Farm

High Low Hall

Veterinary Hospital

Lane End

Geoffrey Schofield Laboratory

Westlakes Science Park

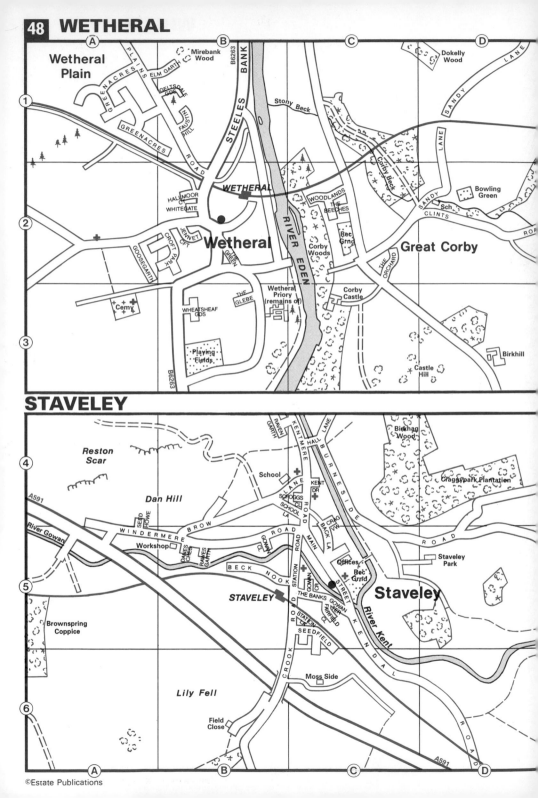

48 WETHERAL

Wetheral Plain

Mirebank Wood

Dokelly Wood

Stony Beck

WETHERAL

Bowling Green

HALLMOOR
WHITEGATE

WOODLANDS
THE BEECHES

Sch

CLINTS

Wetheral

Corby Woods

Rec Grnd

Great Corby

Cemy

THE GLEBE

Wetheral Priory (remains of)

Corby Castle

WHEATSHEAF GDS

Castle Hill

Birkhill

Playing Fields

RIVER EDEN

Corby Beck

SANDY LANE

B6263

STEELES BANK

GREENACRES

PLAINS

ELM GARTH

GELTSDALE GDS

FAUGH HILL

JENNET

CROFT PARK

GOOSEGARTH

THE ORCHARD

STAVELEY

Reston Scar

Birkhag Wood

School

KENT DR

Craggypark Plantation

Dan Hill

SEED HOWE

WINDERMERE

BROW

Workshop

DALES CROFT

RAWES GARTH

BECK NOOK

RAVEN GARTH

KENTMERE LANE

HALL LANE

BURNESIDE ROAD

SCROGGS

SCHOOL LA

CRAG VW

BACK LA

MAIN

STATION ROAD

Offices

Rec Grnd

Staveley Park

Staveley

GOWAN CL

GOWAN LA

THE BANKS

STREET

FAIRFIELD

SEEDFIELD

River Kent

A591

River Gowan

Brownspring Coppice

Lily Fell

CROOK ROAD

STATION ROAD

Moss Side

Field Close

KENDAL

A591

©Estate Publications

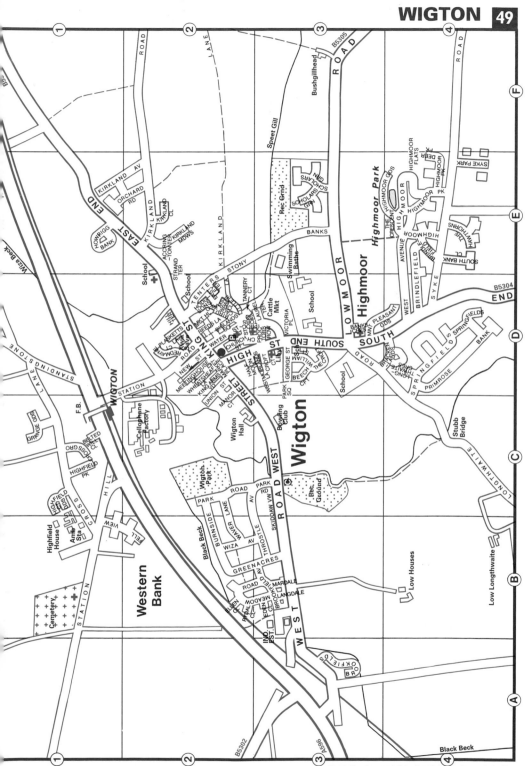

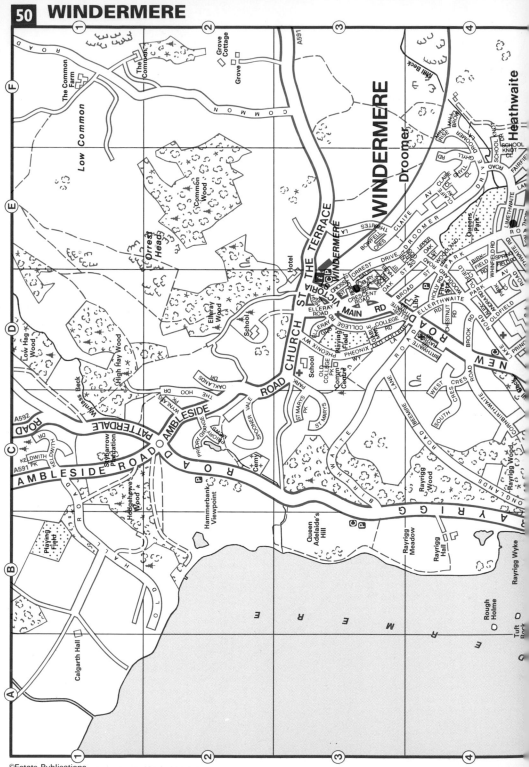

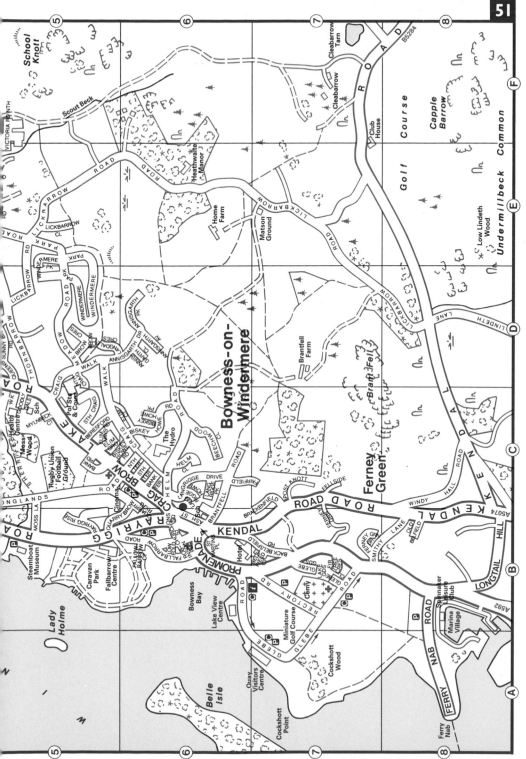

Bowness-on-Windermere

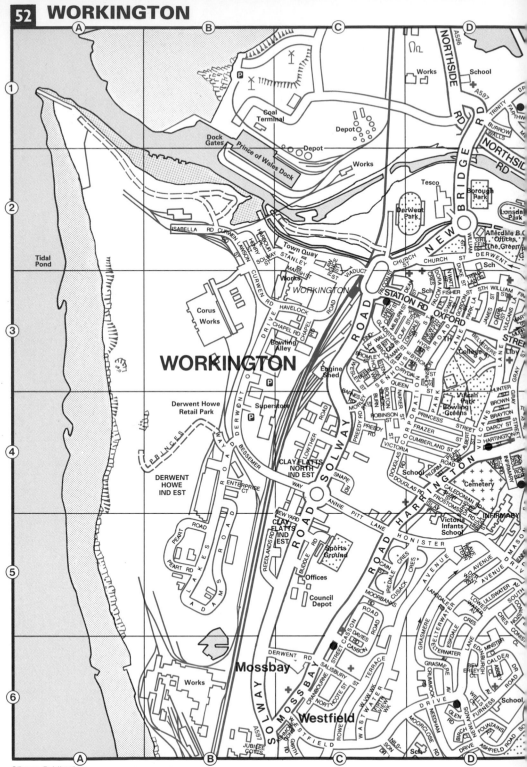

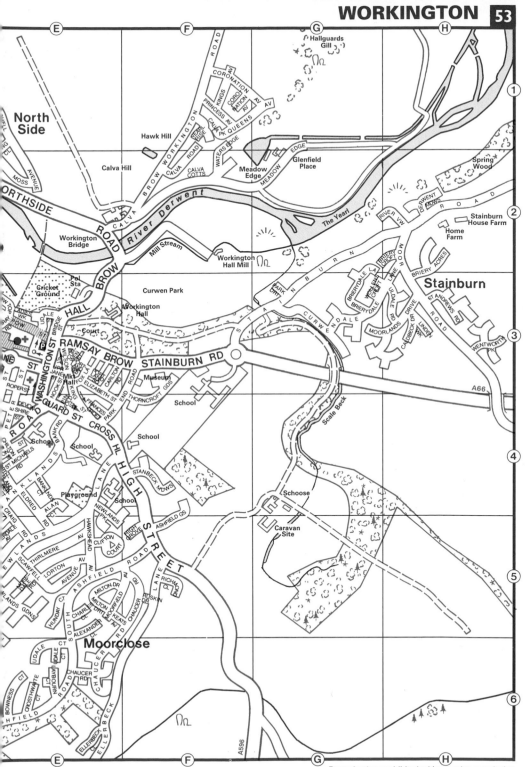

Cows Tarn La. LA14 18 A1
Cragg St. LA14 19 F1
Crellin St. LA14 19 F2
Cross St. LA14 19 F3
Cumbria Vw. LA14 18 B6
Dalkeith St. LA14 19 E2
Dalton St. LA14 19 F2
Darent Av. LA14 18 A3
Dartmouth St. LA14 18 C4
Delhi St. LA14 18 C4
Denton Rd. LA14 19 H1
Derby St. LA13 19 H3
Derry St. LA14 19 G3
Derwent Bank. LA14 18 A2
Devon St. LA13 19 H2
Dominion St. LA14 18 C4
Doncaster Pl. LA13 19 H2
Doris St. LA14 18 C3
Dorset St. LA14 19 F1
Douglas St. LA14 18 C3
Dover St. LA14 18 C4
Drake St. LA14 19 E1
Dryden St. LA14 19 F2
Duddon Dri. LA14 18 A3
Duke St. LA14 19 E2
Dumfries St. LA14 19 G3
Dunbar St. LA14 19 F5
Duncan St. LA14 19 E3
Dundalk St. LA14 19 F5
Dundas St. LA14 19 E1
Dundee St. LA14 19 E4
Dundonald St. LA14 19 E2
Dunoon St. LA14 19 F5
Dunvegan St. LA14 19 F5
Eamont Clo. LA14 18 B2
Earle St. LA14 18 D4
Eden Av. LA14 18 B2
Egerton Ct. LA14 19 F5
Elizabethan Way. LA14 19 F1
Emlyn St. LA14 19 F2
Empress Dri. LA14 18 C4
Eskdale Av. LA13 19 G2
Euryalus St. LA14 18 C4
Ewan Clo. LA13 19 H1
Exmouth St. LA14 19 E1
Falmouth St. LA14 18 B4
Farm St. LA14 19 E4
Fell St. LA14 19 F2
Fenman Clo. LA14 19 G3
Fenton St. LA14 19 F2
Ferry Beach Rd. LA14 18 D3
Ferry Rd. LA14 18 D4
Fife St. LA13 19 G2
*Fishermans Yd,
  Church St. LA14 19 F3
Florence St. LA14 19 G3
Folkestone Av. LA14 18 C4
Forshaw St. LA14 19 F3
Foundry St. LA14 19 G3
Foxfield Rd. LA14 18 C1
Franklin St. LA14 19 E2
Frederick St. LA13 19 H3
French St. LA14 18 C3
Frome Rd. LA14 18 A1
Gatacre St. LA14 18 C3
Gatacre Ter. LA14 18 C3
Gateshead St. LA13 19 G3
Geneva St. LA14 19 F3
Glasgow St. LA14 19 G3
Gloucester St. LA13 19 H2
Goldsmith St. LA14 19 E1
Grange Cres. LA14 19 E2
Granville St. LA14 19 E1
Greengate St. LA14 19 F3
Hannay Clo. LA14 19 E3
Hardwick St. LA14 19 E1
Hardy St. LA14 19 E3
Harley St. LA14 19 F3
Harrison St. LA14 19 F3
Hartington St. LA14 19 E1
Hastings St. LA14 18 C4
Haverigg Gdns. LA14 18 B1
Hawke St. LA14 18 C4
Hempland Av. LA14 19 H1
Hibbert Rd. LA14 19 E2
High St. LA14 19 E2
Himalaya Av. LA14 18 C5
Hindpool Rd. LA14 19 E3
Hogue St
Holcroft Hill. LA13 19 H2
Holker St. LA14 19 E1
Hood St. LA14 19 E2
Hope St. LA14 19 G3
Hornedale Av. LA13 19 G1
Howard St. LA14 19 E2
Howe St. LA14 19 E1

Humber Ter. LA14 18 A1
Ironworks Rd. LA14 18 D2
Irwell Rd. LA14 18 A2
Island Rd. LA14 19 E4
Ivy Av. LA14 18 E4
James Freel Clo. LA14 18 D1
James St. LA14 19 F2
James Watt Ter. LA14 19 E5
Jarrow St. LA13 18 C4
Jason St. LA14 18 C5
Jesmond Av. LA13 19 G1
Jubilee Bri. LA14 18 C4
Juno St. LA14 18 C4
Keith St. LA14 19 E3
Kennet Rd. LA14 18 A2
Kent St. LA13 19 H3
Keppel St. LA14 19 E2
Keyes St. LA14 19 E1
King Alfred St. LA14 18 C5
Kirkby Gdns. LA14 18 C1
Kitchener St. LA14 18 C3
Knox St. LA14 19 E1
Lancaster St. LA14 19 F1
Langdale Gro. LA13 19 G2
Latona St. LA14 18 C3
Laundry St. LA14 19 E3
Lawson Rd. LA14 18 A3
Leicester St. LA13 19 H2
Leighton Dri. LA14 18 C1
Leopard St. LA14 19 E1
Lesh La. LA13 19 H1
Lincoln St. LA14 19 F1
Lindal St. LA14 19 F2
Liverpool St. LA14 18 C4
Long Bank. LA14 18 C5
Longreins Rd. LA14 19 F1
Lord Roberts St. LA14 18 C3
Lord St. LA14 19 F3
Lorne Rd. LA13 19 G2
Lowther Cres. LA14 18 C1
Lumley St. LA14 18 B3
Lyne Clo. LA14 18 B3
Lyon St. LA14 19 E2
Macadam St. LA14 19 G3
Mallard Dri. LA14 18 B5
Manchester St. LA14 19 F2
Mardale Gro. LA13 19 G2
Margate St. LA14 18 C4
Market St. LA14 19 E3
Marsden St. LA14 19 G3
Marsh St. LA14 19 E2
Maryport Av. LA14 18 B3
McClintock St. LA14 19 F2
McLean Pl. LA14 19 F2
Medway Rd. LA14 18 B3
Melampus St. LA14 18 C3
Melbourne St. LA14 19 E1
Mercer St. LA14 19 F3
Mersey Rd. LA14 18 B3
Methuen St. LA14 18 C3
Michaelson Rd 19 E4
Middle Hill. LA13 19 H1
Mikasa St. LA14 18 C4
Mill La. LA14 18 B3
Mill St. LA14 19 F2
Milton St. LA14 19 E2
Monk St. LA14 19 E2
Montague St. LA14 19 E2
Moor Tarn La. LA14 18 A3
Moorfield St. LA13 19 H3
Mosley St. LA14 19 E3
Mount Pleasant. LA14 19 F3
Muncaster Rd. LA14 18 C1
Naiad St. LA14 18 C5
Napier St. LA14 19 E3
Natal Rd. LA14 18 C4
Nelson St. LA14 19 E2
Netherfield Clo. LA14 18 C5
New Leys. LA13 19 H2
New St. LA14 19 G3
Newbarns Rd. LA13 19 G3
Newcastle St. LA13 18 C5
Niger St. LA14 18 C5
Niobe St. LA14 18 C4
North Rd. LA14 18 D3
North Scale. LA14 18 B1
North St. LA13 19 H3
Oak Head Rd. LA14 18 C5
Ocean St. LA14 18 B6
Orion Ter. LA14 18 C5
Oronsay Gdns. LA14 18 B5
Orontes Av. LA14 18 B5
Orsova Gdns. LA14 18 B5
Osborne St. LA14 19 E1
Osprey Dri. LA14 18 B5
Oxen Croft. LA13 19 H2

Parade St. LA14 19 E3
Paradise St. LA14 19 F3
Park Av. LA13 19 F1
Park Dri. LA13 19 G1
Park La. LA14 18 C4
Parker St. LA14 19 F2
Parry St. LA14 19 E2
Paxton St. LA14 19 F3
Penrith St. LA14 19 G3
Peter Green Way. LA14 18 D1
Phoenix Rd. LA14 18 D1
Plymouth St. LA14 18 B5
Portsmouth St. LA14 18 B5
Pottery St. LA14 19 G3
Powerful St. LA14 18 C3
Priors Path. LA13 19 H2
Promenade. LA14 18 C2
Pypers Croft. LA13 19 H2
Raglan St. LA14 19 H3
Raleigh St. LA14 18 C5
Ramsden Dock Rd. LA14 19 E5
Ramsden Sq. LA14 19 E2
Ramsden St. LA14 19 F3
Ramsgate Cres. LA14 18 C4
Rawlinson St. LA14 19 F2
Red Ley La. LA14 18 B1
Ribble Gdns. LA14 18 A3
Risedale Rd. LA13 19 H2
Risingside. LA14 19 H1
Robert St. LA14 19 F2
Roding Grn. LA14 18 B2
Rodney St. LA14 19 E2
Rother Grn. LA14 18 A2
Rutland St. LA14 19 F1
St Andrews St. LA14 19 F5
St Georges Sq. LA14 19 F4
St Lukes Av. LA13 19 H3
St Lukes St. LA13 19 H3
St Patricks Rd. LA14 19 E4
St Quintin Av. LA13 19 H1
Salthouse Rd. LA14 19 F3
Sandy Gap La. LA14 18 A5
Saunders Clo. LA14 18 C2
Schneider Sq. LA14 19 F3
School St. LA14 19 F2
Scott St. LA14 19 F2
Settle St. LA14 19 F1
Severn Rd. LA14 18 A2
Shearwater Cres. LA14 18 B5
Sherwin St. LA14 19 H3
Ship St. LA14 19 E5
Sidney St. LA14 19 E3
Siemens St. LA14 19 E3
Silloth Cres. LA14 18 B2
Silverdale St. LA14 19 F2
Slater St. LA14 19 E2
Sloop St. LA14 19 E5
Smeaton St. LA14 19 G3
Snaefell Vw. LA14 18 B4
Solway Dri. LA14 18 A1
Southampton St. LA14 18 B4
Southport Dri. LA14 18 B4
Springfield Clo. LA14 18 C1
Stafford St. LA14 19 F1
Stanley Rd. LA14 18 D3
Steamer St. LA14 19 E5
Steel St. LA14 19 E2
Stephen St. LA14 19 F3
Stewart St. LA14 18 D3
Storey Sq. LA14 19 F3
Strathaird Av. LA14 18 C5
Strathmore Av. LA14 18 C5
Strathnaver Av. LA14 18 C5
Suffolk St. LA14 19 G2
Sutherland St. LA14 19 F2
Talisman Clo. LA14 19 G3
Tamar Gdns. LA14 18 A1
Teasdale Rd. LA14 18 B1
Tees Gdns. LA14 18 B3
Thames Rd. LA14 18 B3
The Strand. LA14 19 F3
Thwaite St. LA14 19 F3
Tideway Dri. LA14 18 B6
Torridge Dri. LA14 18 A2
Trent Vale. LA14 18 B3
Trinity St. LA14 19 E4
Tweed Rise. LA14 18 B3
Tyne Rd. LA14 18 B3
Vengeance St. LA14 18 C5
Verdun Av. LA14 18 B4
Vernon St. LA14 19 E2
Vincent St. LA14 19 E3
Vulcan Rd. LA14 19 G3
Wallace St. LA14 19 E2
Walney Rd. LA14 18 D2

Walton La. LA13 19 H2
Warren St. LA14 18 C3
Warwick St. LA14 19 F1
Wasdale Gro. LA13 19 G2
Water Garth. LA14 18 B6
Weaver Grn. LA14 18 A2
Webstray Clo. LA14 18 B6
Wensum Lea. LA14 18 A1
West Av. LA13 19 G1
West Shore Rd. LA14 18 A1
West View Rd. LA14 19 F1
Westbourne Cres. LA13 19 G1
Westgate Rd. LA14 19 F1
Westminster Av. LA14 18 C5
Westmorland St. LA14 19 F1
Weymouth St. LA14 18 B4
Whinney End. LA13 19 H2
Whitaker St. LA14 19 F2
Whitehead Clo. LA14 19 F2
Whitehead St. LA14 19 F2
Winchester St. LA13 19 H2
Windrush Cres. LA14 18 A1
Worcester St. LA13 19 H2
Wordsworth St. LA14 19 E1
York St. LA14 19 F1

BRAMPTON

Ash Lea. CA8 20 B2
Back La. CA8 20 A1
Beck La. CA8 20 B2
Beck Orchard. CA8 20 A2
Beckriggs. CA8 20 A2
Beckside Gdns. CA8 20 C2
Berrymoor Rd. CA8 20 B1
Cambeck Clo. CA8 20 B2
Cambeck Rise. CA8 20 B3
Carlisle Rd. CA8 20 A3
Carricks Yd. CA8 20 C2
Church La. CA8 20 C2
Craw Hall. CA8 20 C2
Craw Pk. CA8 20 C2
Croft Rd. CA8 20 B1
Dacre Rd. CA8 20 B1
Elmfield. CA8 20 A3
Falkins Hill. CA8 20 B1
Farish Clo. CA8 20 B1
Front St. CA8 20 B2
Gelt Rise. CA8 20 B3
Gelt Rd. CA8 20 B2
Green Croft. CA8 20 B1
Greenfield La. CA8 20 B1
Greenhill. CA8 20 A3
High Cross St. CA8 20 B2
Howard Arms La. CA8 20 B2
Howard Gdns. CA8 20 B2
Howard Rd. CA8 20 B1

INDUSTRIAL & RETAIL:
Townfoot
  Ind Est. CA8 20 A2
Irthing Pk. CA8 20 B1
Irthing Walk. CA8 20 B2
Jocks Hill. CA8 20 C2
Kingwater Clo. CA8 20 B2
Longtown Rd. CA8 20 A1
Lovers La. CA8 20 C2
Low Cross St. CA8 20 B2
Main St. CA8 20 B2
Manor Gdns. CA8 20 B2
*Mark Ter,
  Main St. CA8 20 B2
Millfield. CA8 20 C2
Moat Side. CA8 20 C2
Moat St. CA8 20 C2
Morpeth Clo. CA8 20 B1
Oak Pk. CA8 20 C2
Old Church La. CA8 20 A1
Oulton Ter. CA8 20 B3
Parkhead. CA8 20 B3
Parkhead Rd. CA8 20 B3
Paving Brow. CA8 20 C3
Ridgevale Ter. CA8 20 C2
St Martins Dri. CA8 20 B2
St Martins Dri. CA8 20 B2
Sawmill La. CA8 20 B1
Showfield. CA8 20 B2
Stanley Rd. CA8 20 B1
Station Rd. CA8 20 C2
*Stephensons La,
  Moat Side. CA8 20 B2
Tarn Rd. CA8 20 B2
The Grove. CA8 20 B2
The Swartle. CA8 20 B2
Townfoot Clo. CA8 20 A2

Townfoot Pk. CA8 20 A2
Tree Gdns. CA8 20 C3
Tree Rd. CA8 20 C5
Tree Ter. CA8 20 C3
Union La. CA8 20 B2
Well Lonning Clo. CA8 20 B2
Wellmeadow. CA8 20 B2

BROUGH

Back La. CA17 20 B4
Black Bull La. CA17 20 C5
Bridge St. CA17 20 C5
Castle Vw. CA17 20 B5
Croft Clo. CA17 20 B5
Helbeck Rd. CA17 20 B4
Leacett La. CA17 20 C6
Market St. CA17 20 B4
Musgrave. CA17 20 A5
New Rd. CA17 20 C5
Upper Market St. CA17 20 C5
Vicarage Dri. CA17 20 B6

CARLISLE

Abbey St. CA3 23 G3
Abbotts Rd. CA2 23 E5
Acredale Rd. CA2 22 A3
Adelphi Ter. CA2 23 H6
Aglionby St. CA1 23 H4
*Albert St,
  Chapel St. CA1 23 H3
Albion St. CA1 23 H5
*Alfred St Nth,
  Portland Sq. CA1 23 H4
*Alfred St Sth,
  Portland Sq. CA1 23 H4
Alton St. CA2 23 H6
Andover Clo. CA2 22 D5
Annetwell St. CA3 23 G3
Archers Garth. CA2 22 D3
Arthur St. CA2 23 H6
Ashley St. CA2 23 E4
Ashman Clo. CA2 23 F6
Atholl Gro. CA2 22 C6
Avon Clo. CA2 22 C5
*Backhouses Wk, Viaduct
  Estate Road. CA3 23 G4
Balfour Rd. CA2 22 D5
Balmoral Ct. CA3 23 G4
Bank St. CA3 23 G4
*Bartons Pl,
  Mary St. CA1 23 H4
Bassenthwaite St. CA2 23 E4
Beaconsfield St. CA2 23 H6
Beaver Rd. CA2 22 B3
Beck Clo. CA2 22 B3
Beck Rd. CA2 22 B3
Bedford Rd. CA2 23 E5
Beech Gro. CA3 23 H1
Belah Rd. CA3 23 E1
Belfry Clo. CA3 23 E1
Bellgarth Gdns. CA2 22 D3
Bellgarth Rd. CA2 22 D3
Bellgarth Rd. CA2 22 D3
Benwell Rd. CA2 22 B4
Berkeley Grange. CA2 22 C4
Beveridge Rd. CA2 23 F6
Birchdale Rd. CA2 22 A4
Birdoswald Dri. CA2 22 A4
Bishops Clo. CA2 23 F4
Blackfriars St. CA3 23 G4
Blencowe St. CA2 23 F5
Blunt St. CA2 23 F4
Borough St. CA3 23 G4
Borrowdale Gdns. CA2 23 E5
Borrowdale Rd. CA2 23 E5
Botchergate. CA1 23 H4
Bousteads Grassing.
  CA2 23 G6
Bower St. CA2 23 E4
Bowscale Clo. CA3 23 F1
Brampton Rd. CA3 23 G2
Bridge La. CA2 23 F3
Bridge Rd. CA2 22 D3
Bridge St. CA2 23 F3
Bridge Ter. CA2 23 G6
Bright St. CA2 23 E4
Broadguards. CA2 23 F4
Brookside. CA2 23 F4
Brookside Pl. CA2 23 E4
Brownrigg Dri. CA2 22 D6

*Brunswick St,
  Warwick Rd. CA1 23 H4
Burgh Rd. CA2 22 A1
Burnrigg. CA2 22 D6
Burnsall Clo. CA2 22 B6
Burnside Ct. CA3 23 G1
*Bush Brow,
  Victoria Viaduct. CA3 23 G4
Buttermere Clo. CA2 23 E5
Byron St. CA2 23 F3
Caldbeck Rd. CA2 23 E4
Caldcotes. CA2 23 F4
Caldew St. CA2 23 G6
Canal Ct. CA2 23 E4
Canal St. CA2 23 F4
Carlton Gdns. CA3 23 G1
Cartmel Dri. CA2 22 B5
Carvoran Way. CA2 22 B4
Castle St. CA3 23 G3
Castle Way. CA3 23 G3
Castlerigg Dri. CA2 22 D6
Castlesteads Dri. CA2 22 A4
Cavendish Ter. CA3 23 G2
Caxton Rd. CA2 22 D3
Cecil St. CA1 23 H4
*Chapel Pl,
  Charlotte St. CA2 23 G4
Chapel St. CA1 23 H3
Charlotte St. CA2 23 H3
Chatsworth Sq. CA1 23 H3
Cherry Brow. CA2 22 C5
Chesterholm. CA2 22 B4
Cheviot Rd. CA3 23 G1
Chiswick St. CA1 23 H4
Church La. CA3 23 G1
Church Pl. CA3 23 G1
Church St,
  Caldewgate. CA2 23 F4
Church St,
  Stanwix. CA3 23 G1
Church Ter. CA3 23 G1
*Citadel Row,
  English St. CA3 23 H4
Clarence St. CA2 23 F6
Clementina Ter. CA2 23 H6
Clift St. CA2 23 E3
Clifton St. CA2 23 F5
Coalfell Av. CA2 22 B4
Cole La. CA2 23 H5
Coledale Mdws. CA2 22 D3
*Colin Pl,
  Newtown Rd. CA2 22 C3
Collingwood St. CA2 23 G5
Colmore St. CA2 23 G6
Colville St. CA2 23 F5
Colville Ter. CA2 23 F5
Compton St. CA1 23 H3
*Conisburgh Ct,
  Elm St. CA2 23 G5
Coniston Way. CA2 22 B5
Constable St. CA2 23 F6
Coogan. CA2 23 F6
Corporation Rd. CA3 23 G3
Court Sq. CA3 23 H4
Cranbourne Rd. CA2 22 D4
Creighton Av. CA2 22 D4
Criffel Rd. CA2 22 B3
Cromwell Cres. CA3 23 G2
Crosby St. CA1 23 H4
Crosshill Dri. CA2 22 C6
Crown Rd. CA2 22 B3
Crown St. CA2 23 H5
Crummock St. CA2 23 E4
*Cumberland Ct,
  Norfolk Rd. CA2 23 E4
*Currie St,
  Chiswick St. CA1 23 H4
Currock Rd. CA2 23 H6
Currock St. CA2 23 H5
Dacre Rd. CA3 23 F3
Dale Ct. CA2 23 F6
Dale St. CA2 23 G6
Dalmeny Rd. CA3 23 G1
Dalston St. CA2 23 E6
Dalston St. CA2 23 G6
Dalton Av. CA2 22 D5
Dee Clo. CA2 22 C6
Denton Mill Clo. CA2 23 F6
Denton Mill La. CA2 23 F6
Denton St. CA2 23 G5
Derwent St. CA2 23 E5
*Devonshire St,
  Lowther St. CA3 23 H4
Devonshire Wk. CA3 23 F3
Diggle Rd. CA2 23 F6
*Dixon St,
  Corporation Rd. CA3 23 G3

Dobinson Rd. CA2 22 C4
Dowbeck Rd. CA2 23 F5
*Drovers La,
  Lowther St. CA3 23 H3
*Drury La,
  Lonsdale St. CA1 23 H4
Duke St. CA2 23 F4
Dukes Rd. CA1 23 H3
Dunmail Dri. CA2 23 E5
Dunmallet Rigg. CA2 22 D6
Dykes Ter. CA3 23 H1
*Earl St,
  Warwick Rd. CA1 23 H4
*Earls La,
  Lonsdale St. CA3 23 H4
East Dale St. CA2 23 G6
East Nelson St. CA2 23 G5
East Norfolk St. CA2 23 G6
*East Tower St,
  Rickergate. CA3 23 G3
Eden Bri. CA3 23 G2
Eden Mount. CA3 23 G1
Eden Pl. CA3 23 F1
Eden St. CA3 23 F1
Egerton Gro. CA2 22 C5
Elm St. CA2 23 G5
Empire Rd. CA2 23 F5
Engine Lonning. CA2 22 D3
*English Damside, Viaduct
  Estate Rd. CA3 23 G4
English St. CA3 23 G4
Eskdale Av. CA2 23 E5
Etterby Lea Cres. CA3 23 G1
Etterby Lea Gro. CA3 23 G1
Etterby Lea Rd. CA3 23 G1
Etterby Rd. CA3 23 E2
Etterby Scaur. CA3 23 F1
Etterby St. CA3 23 G1
Fairfield Gdns. CA2 23 E5
Fellside Gro. CA2 22 C5
Fergus Way. CA2 22 C5
*Ferguson Pl,
  Ferguson Rd. CA2 23 F6
Ferguson Rd. CA2 23 F6
Finkle St. CA2 23 G3
Finn Av. CA2 23 F4
Fisher St. CA3 23 G3
Freer Ct. CA2 23 F6
Freer St. CA2 23 F6
*Friars Ct,
  Lowther St. CA3 23 H4
Fulford Wk. CA3 23 E1
Garden St. CA3 23 F1
Gardenia St. CA2 23 H6
Garfield St. CA2 23 G5
Georgian Way. CA1 23 H3
Gleneagles Dri. CA3 23 E1
Globe La. CA3 23 G3
Goschen Rd. CA2 23 F6
Gosforth Rd. CA2 22 A5
Graham St. CA2 23 G5
Granville Rd. CA2 23 E4
Grapes La. CA3 23 G4
Grasmere St. CA2 23 H6
Green La. CA2 22 A4
Green Mkt. CA3 23 G4
Greta Av. CA2 23 E5
Greystone La. CA3 22 C1
Grinsdale Av. CA2 22 B3
Grosvenor Ct. CA3 23 F1
Grosvenor Pl. CA3 23 F1
Hanover Ct. CA2 22 C5
Hardwicke Circus. CA3 23 G3
Harrison St. CA2 23 H6
Hartington Pl. CA1 23 H4
Hartington St. CA1 23 H3
Harvey St. CA2 22 D3
*Hawes St,
  Bassenthwaite St.
  CA2 23 E5
Hawick St. CA2 23 F4
Hawthorn Gro. CA2 22 C5
Head St. CA2 23 E4
Hebden Av. CA2 22 B6
Hewson St. CA2 23 G5
Heysham Pk Av. CA2 23 E1
Hicks Ter. CA3 23 E1
*Higginson St,
  Denton Mill La. CA2 23 F6
High Meadow. CA2 22 C4
Holme La. CA3 22 C1
Holmes Ter. CA3 23 F4
Holmrook Rd. CA2 22 A5
Hope St. CA2 23 G6
Housesteads Rd. CA2 22 A4
Howard St. CA2 23 E4

Hutton Way. CA2 22 B5

INDUSTRIAL & RETAIL:
Burgh Rd
  Ind Est. CA2 22 B3
Newtown
  Ind Est. CA2 22 C3
Port Rd
  Business Pk. CA2 23 E3
Stephenson
  Ind Est. CA2 23 E2
Willowholme
  Ind Est. CA2 23 E2
Infirmary St. CA2 23 E3
Inglewood Ct. CA2 22 D5
Inglewood Cres. CA2 22 D5
Inglewood Rd. CA2 22 D5
Ivory Clo. CA2 22 D4
James St. CA2 23 G5
*Jane St,
  Willow Holme. CA2 23 F3
John St. CA2 23 F4
Johns Pl. CA2 23 G4
*Johnson Mill,
  Denton Mill Clo. CA2 23 F6
Junction St. CA2 23 F4
Kaye Clo. CA2 22 D6
Keld Rd. CA2 22 B3
Kells Pl. CA3 23 H1
Kelvin Gro. CA2 23 E6
Kendal St. CA2 23 F4
Kenmount Pl. CA2 23 F5
*Kilduff Row,
  Shaddongate. CA2 23 F4
King St. CA1 23 H5
Kingmoor Rd. CA3 23 E1
Kirkstead Clo. CA2 22 A4
Kirkstead Rd. CA2 22 A4
Kirkstone Cres. CA2 23 E5
Kirriemuir Way. CA3 23 E1
Knowe Park Av. CA3 23 H1
Knowe Rd. CA3 23 H1
*Knowe Ter,
  Kells Pl. CA3 23 G1
Lamplugh St. CA2 23 G5
Lancaster St. CA1 23 H5
Langrigg Rd. CA2 23 E6
Langdale Av. CA2 23 E5
Lansdowne Cres. CA3 23 G1
Lawson St. CA2 23 E3
Leatham Rd. CA2 23 E4
Leicester St. CA2 23 F6
Levens Av. CA2 23 E6
Lichen Gro. CA2 22 D4
Lime Gro. CA2 22 D4
Lime St. CA2 23 G5
Lister Ct. CA2 22 D4
Lodore Dri. CA2 22 A5
*Long La,
  Castle St. CA3 23 G3
Lonsdale St. CA1 23 H4
Lord St. CA1 23 H5
Lorne Cres. CA2 23 G5
Lorne St. CA2 23 G5
Low Meadow. CA2 22 C4
*Lowther Browns
  Lonning. CA2 22 D6
Lowther St. CA3 23 H3
*Lowthians La,
  English St. CA3 23 G4
Lytham Clo. CA2 22 C5
Lytham Ct. CA2 22 C5
Marconi Rd. CA2 22 C3
Mardale Rd. CA2 23 E4
Market St. CA3 23 G3
Marks Av. CA2 23 F4
Marlborough Gdns.
  CA3 23 G2
Mary St. CA1 23 H4
Mayors Dri. CA3 23 F3
Metcalfe St. CA2 23 G5
Milbourne St. CA2 23 F4
Miles McInnes Ct. CA3 23 G2
Millrace Rd. CA2 23 E3
*Millrace Vw,
  Denton Mill Clo. CA2 23 F6
Moffat Ter. CA2 23 F5
Monks Close Rd. CA2 23 E4
Moor Park Av. CA2 22 B3
Moorhouse Rd. CA2 22 A3
Morley St. CA2 23 G5
Morton Ct. CA2 22 D6
Morton St. CA2 23 F4
Mortonrigg. CA2 22 D6
Mulcaster Cres. CA3 23 G1
Murrel Hill. CA2 23 F5
Nairn Way. CA2 22 C5

Nelson Bri. CA2 23 G5
Nelson St. CA2 23 F5
Ness Way. CA2 22 C5
Newcastle St. CA2 23 F4
Newlaithes Av. CA2 23 E6
Newmarket Rd. CA2 23 H3
Newton Clo. CA2 22 C3
Newtonrigg. CA2 22 D6
Newtown Clo. CA2 22 C3
Newtown Rd. CA2 22 C3
Nicholson St. CA2 23 H6
Norfolk Ct. CA2 23 G5
Norfolk Rd. CA2 23 E6
Norfolk St. CA2 23 F6
Norfolk Ter. CA2 23 F5
North St. CA2 23 G6
North Vw. CA3 23 H1
Northumberland St.
  CA2 23 G5
Orfeur St. CA1 23 H4
Orton Pl. CA2 22 C5
Orton Rd. CA2 22 A6
Osborne Av. CA2 23 F4
*Packhorse La,
  Lowther St. CA3 23 H4
Palmer Rd. CA2 22 B3
Parham Dri. CA2 22 C4
Parham Gro. CA2 22 C4
Park Rd. CA2 23 E6
Partridge Pl. CA2 22 D5
Paternoster Row. CA3 23 G4
Peel St. CA2 23 E4
Percy Rd. CA2 23 E6
Peter St. CA3 23 G3
Port Rd. CA2 23 E4
Portland Pl. CA1 23 H4
Portland Sq. CA1 23 H4
Powlees La. CA3 22 C1
Prescott Rd. CA2 23 E6
Princess St. CA1 23 H5
Priorwood Clo. CA2 22 A5
Priory Rd. CA2 23 E4
Pugin St. CA2 23 F5
Punton Rd. CA3 23 H1
Queen Av. CA2 23 F4
Queensway. CA2 22 B6
Raffles Av. CA2 22 D5
Railton Gdns. CA2 22 B6
Randall St. CA2 23 F6
Ravenstone Way. CA2 22 B5
Red Bank Sq. CA2 23 H6
Red Bank Ter. CA2 23 H6
Reeth Rd. CA2 22 B5
Richardson St. CA2 23 F6
Richmond Grn. CA2 22 C5
Rickergate. CA3 23 G3
Rigg St. CA2 23 F4
Riverbank Ct. CA3 23 E1
Robert St. CA2 23 H5
Robinson St. CA2 23 H6
Romanby Clo. CA3 23 H1
Rome St. CA2 23 G6
Rose St. CA2 23 H6
Rosebery Rd. CA2 23 G1
*Rosemary La,
  Fisher St. CA3 23 G4
Rudchester Clo. CA2 22 B4
Ruthella St. CA2 23 E3
Rydal St. CA1 23 H5
St Anns Rd. CA3 23 E1
St Augusta Vw. CA3 23 E1
*St Cuthberts La,
  West Walls. CA3 23 H4
St Edmunds Pk. CA2 22 B6
St Georges Cres. CA3 23 G1
St James Av. CA2 23 F5
St James Rd. CA2 23 F6
*St Marys Gate,
  Castle St. CA3 23 G3
St Mellion Clo. CA3 23 G3
St Nicholas St. CA1 23 H5
*St Pauls Sq,
  Lonsdale St. CA1 23 H4
St Pierre Av. CA3 23 E1
*St Stephens St,
  Lamplugh St. CA2 23 G5
Salisbury Rd. CA2 23 H6
Sandsfield Rd. CA2 22 A3
Scaurbank Rd. CA2 23 E1
Scawfell Rd. CA2 23 E5
Scotch St. CA3 23 G4
Scotland Rd. CA3 23 G1
Shaddongate. CA2 23 F4
Shady Gro Rd. CA2 22 D5
Shankly St. CA3 23 G6
Shap Gro. CA2 23 E5

Sheehan Cres. CA2 22 C5
Sheffield St. CA2 23 G5
Silloth St. CA2 23 F4
Skelwith Clo. CA2 23 E5
Skiddaw Rd. CA2 23 E5
Solway Pk. CA2 23 E5
*South George St,
  Water St. CA2 23 H5
South Henry St. CA1 23 H5
South John St. CA2 23 H5
South View Ter. CA1 23 H5
South Western Ter.
  CA2 23 H6
Sowerby Ct. CA2 23 H4
Spencer St. CA1 23 H4
*Spring Gdn La,
  Lowther St. CA3 23 H3
Stainton Rd. CA3 22 D1
Stanhope Rd. CA2 23 H5
Stanwix Bank. CA3 23 G2
Stonegarth. CA2 23 H5
Strand Rd. CA1 23 H3
Strathclyde Av. CA2 22 D4
Strawberry Ter. CA3 23 F1
Sunningdale Clo. CA3 23 H4
Suttle Clo. CA2 22 C6
Tait St. CA1 23 H4
Talbot Rd. CA2 23 F5
Tarraby La. CA3 23 H1
The Crescent. CA1 23 H4
The Maltings. CA2 23 F3
Thirlmere St. CA2 23 H6
Thomas La. CA2 22 C3
Thomas St. CA2 23 G6
Thomlinson Av. CA2 22 C4
Thornton Rd. CA3 23 G1
Trafalgar St. CA2 23 G5
Troutbeck Dri. CA2 22 B5
Ullswater Rd. CA2 23 H6
Vallum Clo. CA3 23 H1
Viaduct Est Rd. CA3 23 F4
Victoria Pl. CA1 23 H3
Victoria Viaduct. CA3 23 G4
Wadsworth Rd. CA2 23 F6
Waldegrave Rd. CA2 23 F6
Wansfell Av. CA2 23 E6
Warwick Rd. CA1 23 H4
Warwick Sq. CA1 23 H4
Warwick St. CA3 23 G3
Wastwater Clo. CA2 23 E5
Water St. CA2 23 H5
Weardale Rd. CA2 23 F6
Well Bank. CA2 23 F6
Well Bank Pl. CA2 23 F6
Well La. CA3 23 H1
West Tower St. CA3 23 G4
West Vale Ct. CA2 23 F6
West Walls. CA3 23 G4
Westmorland St. CA2 23 G5
*Wetheral St,
  Silloth St. CA2 23 F4
Wheatlands. CA2 23 E5
Whernside. CA2 22 B5
Whinlatter Way. CA2 23 E5
Whinnie Ho. Pk. CA2 22 C5
Whinnie Ho. Rd. CA2 22 C5
Wigton Rd. CA2 22 C6
*Wilfred St,
  Cecil St. CA1 23 H4
Willow Holme. CA2 23 E3
Willow Holme Gdns.
  CA2 23 F3
Wilson St. CA2 22 D3
Windermere Rd. CA2 23 E5
Wood St. CA2 23 E4
Wootton Way. CA2 23 F6
Wyvern Clo. CA2 22 D5
Yew Clo. CA2 22 C5
Yewdale Rd. CA2 22 A4
York Rd. CA2 23 G1
York St. CA2 23 F4

CLEATOR MOOR

Aldby Gro. CA25 26 D3
Aldby Pl. CA25 26 D3
Aldby St. CA25 26 C3
Birks Rd. CA25 26 C3
Blind La. CA25 26 A4
Border Av. CA25 26 B2
Bowthorn Rd. CA25 26 A2
Brantwood La. CA25 26 A2
Brierley Rd. CA25 26 C4
Buckle St. CA25 26 C4

Calder Cres. CA25 26 C4
Chrysler Gro. CA25 26 B2
Clayton Av. CA25 26 C4
Coniston Pk. CA25 26 C4
Cragg Rd. CA25 26 C3
Croasdale Pl. CA25 26 D4
Cross North St. CA25 26 C3
Crossfield Rd. CA25 26 A4
Crossings Clo. CA25 26 A3
Crowgarth Clo. CA25 26 B4
Dawson St. CA25 26 C2
Dent Pl. CA25 26 D4
Dent Rd. CA25 26 D3
Dent Sq. CA25 26 D3
Duke St. CA25 26 C3
Earl St. CA25 26 C4
Ehen Pl. CA25 26 D3
Ehen Rd. CA25 26 D3
Ennerdale Rd. CA25 26 C3
Eskdale Clo. CA25 26 B2
Fell Side Flats. CA25 26 D4
Fir Garth. CA25 26 B2
Fletcher St. CA25 26 C3
Frizington Rd. CA25 26 E4
Furnace St. CA25 26 B3
Greenthwaite. CA25 26 C3
Greystone Av. CA25 26 E4
Greystone Pl. CA25 26 D4
Grizedale Clo. CA25 26 A2
Heathcote Pk. CA25 26 C2
Henry St. CA25 26 C3
High St. CA25 26 C3
Highfield Rd. CA25 26 B4
Holden Pl. CA25 26 C4
Hopedene. CA25 26 A1
INDUSTRIAL & RETAIL:
Leaconfield Ind Est.
CA25 26 B2
Jacktrees Cres. CA25 26 C4
Jacktrees Rd. CA25 26 B4
James St. CA25 26 C2
John Colligan Dri.
CA25 26 A2
John Colligan Wk.
CA25 26 B2
Keir Hardie Av. CA25 26 D4
King St. CA23 26 D4
Kinniside Pl. CA25 26 D4
Lansbury Pl. CA25 26 D4
Layfield La. CA25 26 B2
Leconfield St. CA25 26 A2
Litt Pl. CA25 26 B2
Longbarrow. CA25 26 C4
Market St. CA25 26 C3
Meadley Pl. CA25 26 C4
Melbreak Av. CA25 26 C4
Mill Hill. CA25 26 A2
Montreal Av. CA25 26 C4
Montreal Clo. CA25 26 C4
Montreal St. CA25 26 C3
Norbeck Pk. CA25 26 A3
North St. CA25 26 D4
Orchard Pl. CA25 26 D4
Park St. CA26 26 F1
Parkside Rd. CA25 26 D4
Princes St. CA23 26 D4
Priory Dri. CA25 26 C4
Queen St. CA25 26 C3
Red Beck Pk. CA25 26 E4
Red Beck Rd. CA25 26 E4
Rheda Ter. CA25 26 C1
Robert Owen Av. CA25 26 D4
Robert Owen Pl. CA25 26 D4
Roper St. CA3 26 D4
Ruskin Pl. CA25 26 A2
Seaview Pl. CA25 26 D4
Snowdon Av. CA25 26 A2
St Johns Clo. CA25 26 B3
*Stafford Ct, Earl St.
CA25 26 C4
The Crescent. CA25 26 A2
Thompson Clo. CA25 26 C3
Thornfield Clo. CA25 26 C4
Threaplands. CA25 26 B2
Todholes Rd. CA25 26 C4
Towerson St. CA25 26 D4
Trumpet Rd. CA23 26 D4
Union St. CA25 26 C3
Victoria St. CA25 26 C3
Wastwater Clo. CA25 26 B2
Weddicar Gdns. CA25 26 B2
Whinney Hill. CA25 26 A2
Whitehaven Rd. CA25 26 A2
William Morris Av.
CA25 26 D4

Wyndham St. CA25 26 C3

COCKERMOUTH

Albemarle St. CA13 24 C4
Allerdale Gro. CA13 24 C5
Back La. CA13 24 C2
Beckside Clo. CA13 25 F3
Beech La. CA13 25 E2
Belbrigg Lonning. CA13 25 E4
Blencathra Ct. CA13 25 E3
Brackenhill La. CA13 24 C4
Brewery La. CA13 24 D3
Briar Bank. CA13 25 E5
Bridge St. CA13 24 D3
Brigham Rd. CA13 24 A4
Buttermere Clo. CA13 25 F4
Butts Fold. CA13 25 E3
Caldecote Av. CA13 24 D5
Castlegate. CA13 25 E3
Castlegate Dri. CA13 25 E2
Cedar La. CA13 25 E2
Challoner Ct. CA13 24 D4
Challoner St. CA13 24 D3
Cherry La. CA13 25 E3
Cocker La. CA13 25 E3
Cockermouth By-Pass.
CA13 24 A2
Coniston Dri. CA13 25 F4
Croft Side. CA13 24 D3
Crown St. CA13 24 C3
Crummock Av. CA13 25 E4
Culgarth Av. CA13 25 E4
Culgarth Clo. CA13 25 E4
Dale Clo. CA13 24 D5
Dale Vw. CA13 24 D5
Dalton St. CA13 24 C4
Deer Orchard Clo. CA13 25 E3
*Derwent Mill,
Riverside Ter. CA13 24 D3
Derwent St. CA13 24 C3
Derwentside Gdns.
CA13 24 D3
Dovers La. CA13 24 B2
Dunmail Cres. CA13 25 F3
Ennerdale Clo. CA13 25 F3
Etterby Clo. CA13 25 E4
Europe Way. CA13 24 D3
Evening Hill Dri. CA13 24 C5
Fern Bank. CA13 24 D4
Fitz Rd. CA13 24 C4
Fletcher Clo. CA13 24 C3
Friars Wk. CA13 24 A2
Gable Av. CA13 25 F4
Gallowbarrow. CA13 24 D4
Goat Brow. CA13 24 C1
Gote Rd. CA13 24 C2
Grassmoor Av. CA13 25 E3
Greenbank La. CA13 25 E5
Greyrigg Av. CA13 24 D5
Grisedale Pl. CA13 25 F3
Harrot Hill. CA13 24 C4
Harrot Rd. CA13 24 C4
Helvellyn Clo. CA13 25 F3
Henry St. CA13 24 C3
High Sand La. CA13 24 D3
Higham Rd. CA13 25 G2
Highfield Rd. CA13 25 F3
Hill St. CA13 24 C4
Holmewood Av. CA13 24 C4
Holmewood Paddock.
CA13 24 C5
Honister Dri. CA13 25 F4
Horsman St. CA13 24 C3
INDUSTRIAL & RETAIL:
Derwent Mills
Commercial Pk.
CA13 24 D2
Lakeland
Business Pk. CA13 24 C5
*Lowther Went
Shopping Centre,
Main St. CA13 24 D3
Isel Rd. CA13 25 E3
John St. CA13 25 E4
Kirkbank. CA13 25 E3
Kirkfell Av. CA13 25 E3
Kirkgate. CA13 25 E3
Kirkstone Av. CA13 24 C4
Laithwaite Clo. CA13 24 C4
Lamplugh Rd. CA13 24 C4
Lancaster Pl. CA13 24 C4
Langdale Dri. CA13 25 F3
Limetree Cres. CA13 25 E2

Lingfell Av. CA13 25 F3
Linstock Av. CA13 25 E5
Little Mill Clo. CA13 25 E4
Lodge Rd. CA13 25 E4
Longcroft. CA13 25 E4
Lorton Rd. CA13 25 E4
Lorton St. CA13 24 D4
Low Rd. CA13 24 C3
Low Sand La. CA13 24 D3
Loweswater Clo. CA13 25 F4
Lowscales Dri. CA13 25 E5
Mackreth Row. CA13 25 E3
Main St. CA13 24 D3
* Manor Ct,
Wakefield Rd. CA13 24 D3
Market Pl. CA13 25 E3
Market St. CA13 25 E3
Marvejols Pk. CA13 25 E3
Mayo Pk. CA13 24 C4
Mayo St. CA13 24 C4
Meadow Bank Clo.
CA13 25 E4
Meadow Gro. CA13 25 E3
Melbreak Av. CA13 25 E3
Mosser Av. CA13 25 F4
New Rd. CA13 24 D4
New St. CA13 24 D3
Newlands Rd. CA13 24 C4
North Clo. CA13 24 C4
Norwood Dri. CA13 25 E4
Oakleigh Ter. CA13 24 B2
Oaktree Cres. CA13 25 E2
Papcastle Rd. CA13 24 B2
Parklands Dri. CA13 24 C3
Parkside Av. CA13 24 D4
Pinfold Clo. CA13 25 E3
Princes Rd. CA13 24 C4
Printers Ct. CA13 24 D3
Riverdale Dri. CA13 24 D5
Riverside Ter. CA13 24 D3
Romely Pl. CA13 24 C4
Rose Hill. CA13 24 B2
Rose La. CA13 25 E5
Rubby Banks Rd. CA13 25 F3
Rydal Dri. CA13 25 F3
St Helens Clo. CA13 24 C3
St Helens St. CA13 24 C3
St Leonards Clo. CA13 24 C3
Scafell Clo. CA13 25 F3
Simonscales La. CA13 25 E5
Skinner St. CA13 24 D4
Slatefell Dri. CA13 25 F3
South St. CA13 24 D3
Spitaling La. CA13 24 C2
Station Rd. CA13 24 D4
Station St. CA13 24 D3
Strawberry Howe Rd.
CA13 25 F5
Sullart St. CA13 24 D3
Sunscales Av. CA13 25 E3
Swinside Clo. CA13 25 F4
The Green. CA13 25 E3
The Level. CA13 24 D4
The Mount. CA13 24 B2
The Parklands. CA13 24 B4
Thirlmere Av. CA13 25 E4
Towers La. CA13 25 E5
Tweed Mill La. CA13 24 D3
Ullswater Dri. CA13 25 F4
Vale Clo. CA13 24 C5
Vicarage La. CA13 25 E3
Victoria Rd. CA13 25 E4
Violet Bank. CA13 25 E5
Wakefield Rd. CA13 24 C4
Walker Croft. CA13 24 C4
Walker St. CA13 24 C4
Wasdale Clo. CA13 25 F3
Waste Fold Clo. CA13 25 E4
Waste La. CA13 25 E3
Waterloo St. CA13 24 D3
Whinfell St. CA13 25 E4
Whiteside Av. CA13 25 E4
Willow La. CA13 25 E5
Windmill Clo. CA13 25 E4
Windmill La. CA13 25 E4
Woodside Av. CA13 25 F4
Wyndham Row. CA13 24 D3

CONISTON

Barratt Croft. LA21 21 C1
Beck Yeat. LA21 21 C2
Church Beck Clo. LA21 21 B2
Collingwood Clo. LA21 21 C2

Hawkshead Old Rd.
LA21 21 C2
Hellens Ct. LA21 21 C2
INDUSTRIAL & RETAIL:
Lake Rd Est. LA21 21 C3
Lake Rd. LA21 21 B2
Little Moss. LA21 21 C2
Little Moss Clo. LA21 21 C1
Ruskin Av. LA21 21 C2
St Martins Ct. LA21 21 C2
Station Rd. LA21 21 B2
The Garth. LA21 21 C2
Tilberthwaite Av. LA21 21 C2
Yewdale Rd. LA21 21 B2

DALTON-IN-FURNESS

Adgarley Way. LA15 27 C6
Ainslie Dale. LA15 27 C3
Ainslie St. LA15 27 C3
Albert St. LA15 27 C3
Ann St. LA15 27 A4
Ashworth St. LA15 27 C3
Askam Rd. LA15 27 A1
Baldwin Av. LA15 27 A4
Bardsea Clo. LA15 27 B6
Barnes Av. LA15 27 B6
Barrow Rd. LA15 27 A6
Baycliff Dri. LA15 27 B6
Beckside Rd. LA15 27 B4
Billings Rd. LA15 27 A6
Bowness Rd. LA15 27 B6
Brent Av. LA15 27 C5
Briarcliffe Gdns. LA15 27 C3
Broughton St. LA15 27 C3
Buccleuch St. LA15 27 A4
Buttermere Dri. LA15 27 C5
Butts Beck. LA15 27 C3
Calder Dri. LA15 27 B6
Castle St. LA15 27 B4
Cavendish St. LA15 27 B4
Cemetery Hill. LA15 27 B4
Chapel St. LA15 27 B4
Church St. LA15 27 B5
Cleator St. LA15 27 B3
Cobden St. LA15 27 B3
Coniston Av. LA15 27 B5
Coronation Dri. LA15 27 B5
Croft Gdns. LA15 27 A4
Crompton Dri. LA15 27 B6
Dale Ter. LA15 27 C4
Dalton Fields La. LA15 27 B5
Dendron Clo. LA15 27 B6
Devonshire St. LA15 27 B3
Duke St. LA15 27 C5
Dunlin Dri. LA15 27 C5
Egerton Ter. LA15 27 B4
Elliscales Av. LA15 27 A3
Ennerdale Clo. LA15 27 B5
Eskdale Dri. LA15 27 B6
Fair Vw. LA15 27 B3
Fell Croft. LA15 27 B4
Garden Ter. LA15 27 B4
Glenfield Rd. LA15 27 B4
Green La. LA15 27 B5
Greystone La. LA15 27 B4
Greystone Mount. LA15 27 C4
Hall St. LA15 27 B4
Hamilton Ter. LA15 27 B4
Hare Ghyll. LA15 27 D3
Hartington St. LA15 27 B4
High Bank. LA15 27 C3
High Cleator St. LA15 27 B3
Hill Rise. LA15 27 C3
Holker Clo. LA15 27 B6
Holly Gate Rd. LA15 27 B5
Hope St. LA15 27 B3
James Ter. LA15 27 B4
Kestrel Dri. LA15 27 C5
King St. LA15 27 C3
Kings Dri. LA15 27 B4
Lancaster St. LA15 27 B4
Langdale Cres. LA15 27 B6
Leece Dri. LA15 27 B6
Levens Clo. LA15 27 C4
Lindal Clo. LA15 27 B6
Little Fields. LA15 27 B4
Long La. LA15 27 A6
Lord St. LA15 27 C3
Loweswater Ter. LA15 27 B5
Maidenlands Cres.
LA15 27 C3
Market Pl. LA15 27 B4

Market St. LA15 27 B4
Marton Clo. LA15 27 C6
Meadow Gro. LA15 27 C4
Merlin Dri. LA15 27 C5
Mount Pleasant. LA15 27 A4
Mouzell Bank. LA15 27 C3
Myrtle Gro. LA15 27 B4
Myrtle Ter. LA15 27 A4
Napier St. LA15 27 C3
Nelson St. LA15 27 B4
Newton Rd. LA15 27 B6
Nursery Gdns. LA15 27 C4
Pennington Clo. LA15 27 B6
Porter St. LA15 27 C3
Prince St. LA15 27 C3
Queen St. LA15 27 C3
Queens Ter. LA15 27 C4
Rawlinson St. LA15 27 B4
Rowlinson Pl. LA15 27 B4
Romney Av. LA15 27 A4
Romney Pk. LA15 27 A3
Romney Rd. LA15 27 A4
Ruskin Av. LA15 27 B5
Rusland Dri. LA15 27 B5
Rydal Clo. LA15 27 B5
St. Helens. LA15 27 A3
Sanderling La. LA15 27 C5
Scales Clo. LA15 27 B6
Siskin Av. LA15 27 C4
Skeldene Clo. LA15 27 A4
Skelgate. LA15 27 A4
Skelwith Dri. LA15 27 B6
Slater St. LA15 27 C3
Stafford St. LA15 27 C3
Stainton Dri. LA15 27 B4
Station Clo. LA15 27 B4
Station Rd. LA15 27 B4
Stone Fold. LA15 27 B5
Tantabank Rd. LA15 27 C4
Thirlmere Clo. LA15 27 B5
Thornton Pk. LA15 27 B6
Tudor Sq. LA15 27 C4
Ullswater Clo. LA15 27 C5
Ulverston Rd. LA15 27 B4
Union St. LA15 27 B4
Urswick Rd. LA15 27 D3
Victoria St. LA15 27 C3
Wellington St. LA15 27 B4
William Clo. LA15 27 C3
Windermere Clo. LA15 27 B5
Yarl Well. LA15 27 C4

EGREMONT

Ashlea Rd. CA22 28 A2
Ashley Gro. CA22 28 A3
Ashley Way. CA22 28 B3
Bank La. CA22 28 C2
Baybarrow Rd. CA22 28 A2
Beck Grn. CA22 28 C2
Beck Side. CA22 28 C2
Beech Av. CA22 28 B1
Braithwaite Ct. CA22 28 C2
Bridge End. CA22 28 C3
Bridge End Pk. CA22 28 C3
Briscoe Rd. CA22 28 C1
Castle Clo. CA22 28 C3
Castle Vw. CA22 28 B3
Castle Wk. CA22 28 C2
Central Av. CA22 28 B2
Chapel St. CA22 28 C2
Chaucer Av. CA22 28 B2
Church St. CA22 28 C2
Coleridge Dri. CA22 28 B2
Cop La. CA22 28 A6
Copeland Av. CA22 28 B1
Cringlethwaite Ter.
CA22 28 D3
Croadalla Av. CA22 28 C2
Croft Ter. CA22 28 C2
Cross Side. CA22 28 C2
Daleview Clo. CA22 28 B4
Daleview Gdns. CA22 28 B4
Dent Rd. CA22 28 C5
Dryden Way. CA22 28 B2
East Rd. CA22 28 C1
Ehen Ct Rd. CA22 28 C2
Ehen Rd. CA22 28 C6
Fair View. CA22 28 A2
Fell Vw Dri. CA22 28 B3
*Garth Bank,
Sunnyside. CA22 28 B2
Gillfoot Av. CA22 28 B1
Gillfoot Rd. CA22 28 B1

Kilner Clo. LA9	31 F4	Robby Lea Dri. LA9	33 E6	Wattsfield La. LA9	32 D2	Poplar St. CA12	34 D4	Manor Ct. CA17	37 B4

Kilner Clo. LA9 — 31 F4
Kirkbarrow. LA9 — 30 D6
Kirkbie Grange. LA9 — 31 E5
Kirkland. LA9 — 30 D6
Langdale Cres. LA9 — 31 F3
Lansdown Clo. LA9 — 33 F1
Larch Gro. LA9 — 31 F5
Levens Clo. LA9 — 33 E2
Library Rd. LA9 — 30 D4
Lingmoor Rise. LA9 — 33 F1
Linnet Gro. LA9 — 33 F2
Little Aynam. LA9 — 31 E5
Littledale. LA9 — 33 G1
Long Clo. LA9 — 30 C6
Longlands Vw. LA9 — 31 F3
Longmeadow La. LA9 — 33 E6
Longpool. LA9 — 31 E4
Loughrigg Av. LA9 — 33 E2
Lound Dri. LA9 — 30 D6
Lound Sq. LA9 — 33 E1
Lound St. LA9 — 31 E6
Low Fellside. LA9 — 30 C4
Low Garth. LA9 — 30 C2
Low Mead. LA9 — 30 C2
*Lower Castle Pk,
 Castle Pk. LA9 — 31 E4
Lowther Pk. LA9 — 31 F5
Lowther St. LA9 — 30 D5
Lumley Rd. LA9 — 32 C2
Lynngarth Dri. LA9 — 30 C5
Maple Dri. LA9 — 30 B6
Market Pl. LA9 — 30 D4
Maude St. LA9 — 30 D4
*Maudes Mdw,
 Town Vw. LA9 — 30 D4
Mayfield Dri. LA9 — 33 F1
Meadow Rd. LA9 — 32 C2
Mealbank Rd. LA9 — 31 F1
Michaelson Rd. LA9 — 32 C1
Middle La. LA9 — 30 D4
Mill Yd. LA9 — 33 E3
Milnthorpe Rd. LA9 — 32 C3
Mint Bridge Rd. LA9 — 31 E2
Mint Clo. LA9 — 31 E3
Mint Dale. LA9 — 31 E3
Mint St. LA9 — 31 E3
Mintsfeet Rd. LA9 — 30 D4
Mintsfeet Rd Nth. LA9 — 30 D2
Mintsfeet Rd Sth. LA9 — 30 D3
Moorefield Clo. LA9 — 30 C1
Moss Ghyll. LA9 — 30 C2
Mount Pleasant. LA9 — 30 C5
Mount St. LA9 — 30 C5
Murley Moss. LA9 — 33 F2
Murley Moss La. LA9 — 33 E2
Natland Mill Beck La.
 LA9 — 33 E2
Natland Rd. LA9 — 33 E2
Nether St. LA9 — 31 E6
New Inn Yd. LA9 — 30 D5
New Rd. LA9 — 30 D5
*New Shambles,
 Market Pl. LA9 — 30 D4
Newbiggin. LA9 — 30 B2
Northgate. LA9 — 31 F4
Oak Tree Rd. LA9 — 31 G5
Oak Wood. LA9 — 30 C6
Old Lound. LA9 — 33 E1
Old Shambles. LA9 — 30 D5
Overdale Clo. LA9 — 30 C2
Oxenholme La. LA9 — 33 E6
Oxenholme Rd. LA9 — 33 E2
Park Av. LA9 — 32 D1
Park Clo. LA9 — 33 E5
Park Side Rd. LA9 — 31 E6
Park St. LA9 — 32 D1
Parkside Cres. LA9 — 31 E6
Parkside Mdw. LA9 — 31 F6
Parr St. LA9 — 31 E5
Peat La. LA9 — 31 F4
Pembroke Ct. LA9 — 32 C1
*Peppercorn La,
 Kirkland. LA9 — 30 D6
Pine Clo. LA9 — 33 F1
Queen Katherine St.
 LA9 — 31 E5
Queen Katherines Av.
 LA9 — 31 E2
Queen St. LA9 — 30 C5
Queens Rd. LA9 — 30 C4
Red Tarn Rd. LA9 — 33 F3
Redmaynes Yd. LA9 — 30 D4
Rinkfield. LA9 — 33 E2
*Rinteln Sq,
 Stricklandgate. LA9 — 30 D4
River Bank Rd. LA9 — 32 C3

Robby Lea Dri. LA9 — 33 E6
Rock Vw. LA9 — 30 D5
Romney Av. LA9 — 32 D1
Romney Gdns. LA9 — 32 D1
Romney Rd. LA9 — 32 D1
Romney Villas. LA9 — 32 D1
Rosemede Av. LA9 — 31 E2
Rowantree Cres. LA9 — 31 G5
Ruskin Clo. LA9 — 33 E2
Rusland Pk. LA9 — 31 F5
Rydal Mount. LA9 — 30 D3
Rydal Rd. LA9 — 31 F5
St Georges Wk. LA9 — 31 E4
St Marks Fold. LA9 — 33 E6
Sandes Av. LA9 — 30 D4
Sandes Ct. LA9 — 30 D4
Sandgate. LA9 — 31 E4
Sandylands Rd. LA9 — 31 E3
Sawmill Clo. LA9 — 31 F4
Sawmill La. LA9 — 31 F4
Scafell Dri. LA9 — 33 F2
Scar View Rd. LA9 — 33 F5
Scroggs La. LA9 — 32 C3
Sedbergh Dri. LA9 — 31 F4
Sedbergh Rd. LA9 — 31 F4
Sedgewick Rd. LA9 — 33 E6
Sedgwick Ct. LA9 — 32 C2
Sepulchre La. LA9 — 30 C4
Serpentine Rd. LA9 — 30 C5
Shanny La. LA9 — 33 E5
Shap Rd. LA9 — 31 E3
Silver Howe Clo. LA9 — 33 F1
Silverdale Dri. LA9 — 31 F5
Singleton Pk Rd. LA9 — 31 G6
Smithy Clo. LA9 — 33 E6
South Rd. LA9 — 30 D6
*South View La,
 Windermere Rd. LA9 — 30 C4
Sparrowmire La. LA9 — 30 C2
Spital Pk. LA9 — 31 E3
*Spring Bank,
 Charles St. LA9 — 30 D3
*Spring Gdns,
 Low Fellside. LA9 — 30 D4
Stainbank Rd. LA9 — 30 C6
Station La. LA9 — 31 E4
Stockbeck. LA9 — 31 E4
Stockgate. LA9 — 31 E4
Stonebank La. LA9 — 30 B6
Stonecross Gdns. LA9 — 30 C1
Stonecross Grn. LA9 — 32 D2
Stonecross Rd. LA9 — 32 C2
Stoney La,
 Hallgarth. LA9 — 30 C2
*Stoney La,
 Serpentine Rd,
 Kendal. LA9 — 30 C4
Stramongate. LA9 — 30 D4
Strickland Ct. LA9 — 30 C3
Stricklandgate. LA9 — 30 D4
*Summerhill Gdns,
 Greenside. LA9 — 30 C5
Sunnyside. LA9 — 31 E5
Swallow Clo. LA9 — 33 G2
*Tanners Yd,
 Highgate. LA9 — 30 D5
Tarn Clo. LA9 — 33 F2
Tealbeck. LA9 — 33 F2
*Tenterfell Ct,
 High Tenterfell. LA9 — 30 C5
The Court. LA9 — 30 D4
Thirlmere Rd. LA9 — 31 G4
Thornleigh Rd. LA9 — 32 D2
Thorny Hills. LA9 — 31 E4
Town End Ct. LA9 — 33 E6
Town Vw. LA9 — 30 D4
Ullswater Rd. LA9 — 31 G4
Underbarrow Rd. LA9 — 30 A5
Undercliff Rd. LA9 — 30 C3
Underley Av. LA9 — 30 C3
Underley Hill. LA9 — 30 C3
Underley Rd. LA9 — 30 C3
Underwood. LA9 — 30 C6
Union St. LA9 — 30 D3
Valley Clo. LA9 — 33 F2
Valley Rd. LA9 — 33 F2
Vicarage Dri. LA9 — 32 C1
Vicars Flds. LA9 — 30 C6
Vicars Garth. LA9 — 30 D6
Vicars Hill. LA9 — 32 D1
Vicars Wk. LA9 — 30 D6
Vine Rd. LA9 — 31 E3
Wandales La. LA9 — 33 F2
Wansfell Dri. LA9 — 33 E2
Wasdale Clo. LA9 — 33 E1
Wattsfield Av. LA9 — 32 D2

Wattsfield La. LA9 — 32 D2
Wattsfield Rd. LA9 — 32 D2
*Weavers Ct,
 Queen Katherine St.
 LA9 — 31 E5
Websters Yd. LA9 — 30 D5
Well Ings. LA9 — 30 C6
West St. LA9 — 32 D1
Westgate. LA9 — 31 E4
Westwood Av. LA9 — 32 C1
Whinfell Dri. LA9 — 31 F3
Whinlatter Dri. LA9 — 33 F3
White Moss. LA9 — 30 C1
Whitebarrow Clo. LA9 — 31 G4
*Whitehorse Yd,
 Stricklandgate. LA9 — 30 D4
Whitestiles. LA9 — 31 E2
Whitton Ter. LA9 — 31 E5
Wildman St. LA9 — 31 E4
Willow Dri. LA9 — 31 F5
Wilson St. LA9 — 31 E6
Windermere Rd.
 LA9 — 30 A1
Woodgate. LA9 — 30 D4
Woolpack Yd. LA9 — 30 D4
Wordsworth Dri. LA9 — 33 E2
Wray Cres. LA9 — 33 F1
Yealand Cres. LA9 — 31 F6
Yeats Clo. LA9 — 32 C2

KESWICK

Acorn St. CA12 — 35 E4
Ambleside Rd. CA12 — 35 E5
Ashtree Av. CA12 — 34 C3
Bank St. CA12 — 34 D4
Blencathra St. CA12 — 35 E4
Borrowdale Rd. CA12 — 35 E4
Brackenrigg Dri. CA12 — 35 F4
Brandlehow Cres. CA12 — 35 F4
Briar Rigg. CA12 — 34 D2
Bridge Ter. CA12 — 34 D3
Brundholme Gdns.
 CA12 — 35 E3
Brundholme Rd. CA12 — 35 E3
Castle La. CA12 — 35 H5
Castlehead Clo. CA12 — 35 E5
Chestnut Hill. CA12 — 35 G4
Church La. CA12 — 34 C2
Church St. CA12 — 35 E4
Crosthwaite Gdns.
 CA12 — 35 E3
Crosthwaite Rd. CA12 — 34 D3
Crow Park Rd. CA12 — 34 D4
Derwent Clo. CA12 — 34 D4
Derwent St. CA12 — 34 D4
Eleven Trees. CA12 — 35 G3
Elliott Park Rd. CA12 — 35 F5
Elm Ct. CA12 — 34 D4
Eskin St. CA12 — 35 E4
Fenton. CA12 — 35 F4
Fieldside Clo. CA12 — 35 G3
Forge La. CA12 — 35 G3
George St. CA12 — 35 E4
Glebe Clo. CA12 — 34 C2
Grange Pk. CA12 — 35 F4
Greta St. CA12 — 35 E4
Grizedale Clo. CA12 — 35 E4
Halls Mead. CA12 — 35 F5
Heads La. CA12 — 34 D4
Heads Mt. CA12 — 34 D4
Heads Rd. CA12 — 34 D4
Helvellyn St. CA12 — 35 E4
High Hill. CA12 — 34 D4
High Portinscale. CA12 — 34 A3
High St. CA12 — 35 E4
Howe La. CA12 — 34 A3
Howraths Ct. CA12 — 34 D4
Lake Rd. CA12 — 34 D4
Lakeland Pk. CA12 — 35 F5
Larch Gro. CA12 — 35 G3
Latrigg Clo. CA12 — 35 F3
Leonard St. CA12 — 35 E4
Limepots Rd. CA12 — 34 D3
Lonscale Vw. CA12 — 35 G3
Lonsties. CA12 — 35 G4
Main St. CA12 — 34 D4
Manesty Vw. CA12 — 35 F4
Manor Brow. CA12 — 35 E5
Manor Pk. CA12 — 35 E4
Market Pl. CA12 — 34 D4
Millfield Gdns. CA12 — 35 F4
Otley Rd. CA12 — 34 D3
Penrith Rd. CA12 — 35 E4

Poplar St. CA12 — 34 D4
Ratcliffe Pl. CA12 — 35 E4
Rickerby La. CA12 — 34 A4
Riverside Ct. CA12 — 34 C4
Rogerfield. CA12 — 35 F5
St Herbert St. CA12 — 35 E4
St Johns St. CA12 — 34 D4
St Kentigern Clo. CA12 — 34 D3
Shorley La. CA12 — 35 E4
Skiddaw St. CA12 — 35 E4
Southey La. CA12 — 34 D3
Southey St. CA12 — 34 D4
Spoonygreen La. CA12 — 35 E2
Springs Garth. CA12 — 35 F5
Springs Rd. CA12 — 35 E5
Standish St. CA12 — 34 D4
Stanger St. CA12 — 34 D4
Station Av. CA12 — 35 E3
Station Rd. CA12 — 35 E4
Station St. CA12 — 35 E4
The Crescent. CA12 — 34 D4
The Hawthorns. CA12 — 35 G3
The Headlands. CA12 — 34 D4
The Heads. CA12 — 34 D4
The Seams. CA12 — 34 D4
Tithebarn St. CA12 — 34 D4
Trinity Way. CA12 — 35 F4
Vicarage Hill. CA12 — 34 D4
Victoria St. CA12 — 34 D4
Windebrowe Av. CA12 — 35 F4
Wordsworth St. CA12 — 35 E4

KIRKBY LONSDALE

Abbotsgate. LA6 — 36 B2
Back La. LA6 — 36 C2
Bective Rd. LA6 — 36 C2
Bentinck Dri. LA6 — 36 B2
Biggins La. LA6 — 36 A3
Biggins Rd. LA6 — 36 B2
Binfold Croft. LA6 — 36 B2
Bridge Brow. LA6 — 36 C3
Chapel Ho La. LA6 — 36 D4
Chapel La. LA6 — 36 C2
Church St. LA6 — 36 B2
Dodgson. LA6 — 36 B2
Fair Vw. LA6 — 36 B1
Fairbank. LA6 — 36 B1
Fairgarth Dri. LA6 — 36 B1
Harling Bank. LA6 — 36 B1
Horse Mk. LA6 — 36 C2
Jingling La. LA6 — 36 C2
Kendal Rd. LA6 — 36 A2
Kitty Gill La. LA6 — 36 A2
Laitha La. LA6 — 36 D4
Leyfield Ct. LA6 — 36 C3
Lune Clo. LA6 — 36 D4
Lunefield Dri. LA6 — 36 C2
Main St. LA6 — 36 C2
Market Sq. LA6 — 36 C2
Market St. LA6 — 36 C2
Mill Brow. LA6 — 36 C2
Milestone Ho. LA6 — 36 C2
Mitchelgate. LA6 — 36 C2
New Rd. LA6 — 36 B2
Pit La. LA6 — 36 A3
Queens Sq. LA6 — 36 C2
Ray Garth. LA6 — 36 B1
Raygarth La. LA6 — 36 A1
Ruskin Dri. LA6 — 36 C2
Salt Pie La. LA6 — 36 B1
Tram La. LA6 — 36 C2
Vicarage La. LA6 — 36 C2

KIRKBY STEPHEN

Appleby Rd. CA17 — 37 B1
Blackgap La. CA17 — 37 D1
Bloody Bones La. CA17 — 37 B3
Brougham La. CA17 — 37 B4
Christian Head. CA17 — 37 D2
Common La. CA17 — 37 B3
Croft St. CA17 — 37 B3
Croglam Rd. CA17 — 37 A5
Faraday Rd. CA17 — 37 B4
Fletcher Hill Pk. CA17 — 37 C3
Hartley La. CA17 — 37 D3
Hartley Rd. CA17 — 37 C3
High St. CA17 — 37 B4
Hobsons La. CA17 — 37 B2
Kirkbank La. CA17 — 37 C1

Manor Ct. CA17 — 37 B4
Market Sq. CA17 — 37 C3
Market St. CA17 — 37 C3
Mellbecks. CA17 — 37 C3
Mill La. CA17 — 37 C3
Nateby Rd. CA17 — 37 B5
North Rd. CA17 — 37 B2
Quarry Clo. CA17 — 37 B5
Redmayne Rd. CA17 — 37 B3
Rowgate. CA17 — 37 B5
Silver St. CA17 — 37 B3
South Rd. CA17 — 37 B4
Station Rd. CA17 — 37 B5
Stoneshot. CA17 — 37 C3
The Court. CA17 — 37 B4
The Crescent. CA17 — 37 C4
Victoria Sq. CA17 — 37 C4
Westgarth Av. CA17 — 37 B4
Westgarth Gate. CA17 — 37 B4
Westgarth Gro. CA17 — 37 B4
Westgarth Rd. CA17 — 37 B4

LONGTOWN

Albert St. CA6 — 36 C6
Arthuret Dri. CA6 — 36 C6
Arthuret Rd. CA6 — 36 C6
Bank St. CA6 — 36 B5
Bellsfield. CA6 — 36 D5
Brampton Rd. CA6 — 36 C6
Briar Lea Ct. CA6 — 36 D6
Bridge St. CA6 — 36 B5
Burn St. CA6 — 36 C6
Carlisle Rd. CA6 — 36 C6
Claremont Dri. CA6 — 36 D5
Dukes Wood Rd. CA6 — 36 D5
English St. CA6 — 36 C5
Esk Bank. CA6 — 36 B5
Esk St. CA6 — 36 C5
Graham St. CA6 — 36 C5
Gretna Rd. CA6 — 36 A5
High St. CA6 — 36 C5
INDUSTRIAL & RETAIL:
 Borders Business Pk.
 CA6 — 36 C6
 Longtown Ind Est.
 CA6 — 36 C6
Ladyseat. CA6 — 36 D5
Langholm Rd. CA6 — 36 A4
Liddel Rd. CA6 — 36 D4
Lochinvar Clo. CA6 — 36 D4
Lovers La. CA6 — 36 D4
Mallsknowe. CA6 — 36 C5
Mary Ct. CA6 — 36 C5
Mary St. CA6 — 36 C5
Mill St. CA6 — 36 C6
Moor Cres. CA6 — 36 D5
Moor Rd. CA6 — 36 D5
Netherby Rd. CA6 — 36 C4
Netherby St. CA6 — 36 C5
Old Rd. CA6 — 36 D5
Powdrake Cres. CA6 — 36 C4
Raefield. CA6 — 36 C5
Stackbraes Rd. CA6 — 36 D5
Swan St. CA6 — 36 C5
The Scaur. CA6 — 36 C5
The Square. CA6 — 36 D4
Ward St. CA6 — 36 C5

MARYPORT

*Ada St,
 Ellenborough Rd.
 CA15 — 38 E3
Alauna Dri. CA15 — 38 C1
Alder Av. CA15 — 38 D3
Alne Rd. CA15 — 38 E3
Ash Clo. CA15 — 38 E3
Ashby St. CA15 — 38 B1
Bank St. CA15 — 38 B1
Bank Ter. CA15 — 38 B3
Beechwood Clo. CA15 — 38 D3
Bounty Av. CA15 — 38 C4
Bradbury Av. CA15 — 38 D3
Bridge St. CA15 — 38 B2
Brook Side. CA15 — 38 B2
Brooklands Av. CA15 — 38 D3
Brow St. CA15 — 38 B2
Buchanan Ter. CA15 — 38 E3
Buttermere Rd. CA15 — 38 B2
Camp St. CA15 — 38 C1
Catherine St. CA15 — 38 B2

59

Cedar Cres. CA15 38 E3
Cherrytree Dri. CA15 38 D3
Christian St. CA15 38 C1
Church St. CA15 38 C2
Church Ter. CA15 38 D3
*Churchill Pl,
  Nelson St. CA15 38 B2
Collins Ter. CA15 38 B4
Coronation St. CA15 38 B3
Crerar Clo. CA15 38 D4
Criffel Av. CA15 38 C1
Crosby St. CA15 38 B2
Crummock Rd. CA15 38 D4
Curzon St. CA15 38 B3
Derwent Av. CA15 38 C3
Eaglesfield St. CA15 38 B2
Edinburgh Rd. CA15 38 C4
Elbra Farm Clo. CA15 38 E3
Elizabeth St. CA15 38 D3
Ellen Ct. CA15 38 D3
*Ellen Villa,
  Ellenborough Rd.
  CA15 38 E3
Ellenborough Old Rd.
  CA15 38 D3
Ellenborough Pl. CA15 38 B3
Ellenborough Rd. CA15 38 D3
Ellenfoot Dri. CA15 38 D4
Ennerdale Rd. CA15 38 C4
Ewanrigg Brow. CA15 38 D4
Ewanrigg Rd. CA15 38 B3
Festival Cres. CA15 38 D4
*Fleming Pl,
  Fleming St. CA15 38 C2
Fleming Sq. CA15 38 C2
Fleming St. CA15 38 C2
Fletcher Cres. CA15 38 D4
Furnace La. CA15 38 B2
Furnace Rd. CA15 38 B2
Galloway Clo. CA15 38 E4
Garner Rd. CA15 38 D4
Gavel St. CA15 38 B3
George St. CA15 38 B2
Gillbeck Pk. CA15 38 E3
Gilmour St. CA15 38 B3
*Grange Villas,
  Main St. CA15 38 D4
Grasmere Ter. CA15 38 D4
Grasslot. CA15 38 B4
Grasslot St. CA15 38 B3
Greenwood Ter. CA15 38 D3
Hawthorn Av. CA15 38 D2
High St. CA15 38 B2
Hillside Clo. CA15 38 E3
Hutton Pl. CA15 38 A3
INDUSTRIAL & RETAIL:
  Glasson
  Ind Est. CA15 38 A3
  Solway Ind Est. CA15 38 B4
Ingleby Ter. CA15 38 C1
*Inglis Ct,
  Main St. CA15 38 D4
Ismay Clo. CA15 38 D4
Ismay Wharf. CA15 38 B2
James St. CA15 38 D3
Jane St. CA15 38 D3
John St. CA15 38 B2
Jubilee Ter. CA15 38 B3
King St. CA15 38 B2
*Kings Ct,
  King St. CA15 38 B2
Kirkby St. CA15 38 B2
Laburnum Gro. CA15 38 D2
*Lancaster Ter,
  Sandy Lonning.
  CA15 38 D3
Lawson St. CA15 38 C2
Lime Gro. CA15 38 E3
Little Camp St. CA15 38 B1
Lower Church St. CA15 38 C2
Loweswater Rd. CA15 38 D4
Macan St. CA15 38 C1
McCarron Ct. CA15 38 B2
Main Rd. CA15 38 A4
Main St. CA15 38 B2
Maple Clo. CA15 38 E3
Marina Rd. CA15 38 A3
Meadow Clo. CA15 38 D3
Meadow Way. CA15 38 D4
Melbreak Av. CA15 38 D4
Mill St. CA15 38 B3
Moorside Dri. CA15 38 C2
Mosedale Cres. CA15 38 C4
Mulgrew Clo. CA15 38 E4
Nelson St. CA15 38 B2

Nether Vw. CA15 38 D3
New Bridge St. CA15 38 B3
North Quay. CA15 38 B2
North St. CA15 38 C1
Oakland Av. CA15 38 D3
*Park Ter,
  Church St. CA15 38 C3
Peart St. CA15 38 C3
Pecklewell La. CA15 38 D4
Pecklewell Ter. CA15 38 D4
Pigeonwell Lonning.
  CA15 38 C1
Pinewood Dri. CA15 38 E3
Pitcairn Cres. CA15 38 D4
Princess Dri. CA15 38 C4
Queen St. CA15 38 B2
Queens Av. CA15 38 C4
Railway Ter. CA15 38 D3
Ritson Wharf. CA15 38 B2
Roper St. CA15 38 B4
Ropery St. CA15 38 B3
Rydal Av. CA15 38 D3
*St Georges Pl,
  George St. CA15 38 B2
Salmoor Rd. CA15 38 A3
Sandy Lonning. CA15 38 D3
School Clo. CA15 38 C3
Scotts Brow. CA15 38 D3
Selby Ter. CA15 38 D2
Senhouse St. CA15 38 B2
*Sewells Yd,
  Crosby St. CA15 38 B2
Shipping Brow. CA15 38 B2
Short Acres. CA15 38 C3
Skiddaw Av. CA15 38 C1
Solway Ter. CA15 38 B2
South Quay. CA15 38 B2
Spring Field Rd. CA15 38 D3
Station St. CA15 38 C2
Steer Av. CA15 38 D3
Strand St. CA15 38 B2
Sycamore Rd. CA15 38 D3
The Arches. CA15 38 C4
The Beeches. CA15 38 D2
The Netherdales. CA15 38 D3
The Promenade. CA15 38 B1
Thirlmere Rd. CA15 38 D4
Ullswater Rd. CA15 38 C4
*Victoria Ter,
  Ellenborough Rd.
  CA15 38 C3
Victory Cres. CA15 38 C3
Wallace La. CA15 38 D3
Ward St. CA15 38 D3
Well La. CA15 38 B2
*West St,
  Nelson St. CA15 38 B2
White Croft. CA15 38 A4
White Croft Ct. CA15 38 B4
White Star Way. CA25 38 A3
William St. CA15 38 C2
Windermere Av. CA15 38 D3
Wood St. CA15 38 B2
Woodlands Dri. CA15 38 D2

MILLOM

Albert St. LA18 39 D2
Argyle St. LA18 39 D3
Bankside. LA18 39 C2
Bassenthwaite Clo.
  LA18 39 C3
Bay Vw. LA18 39 C3
Bedford St. LA18 39 E3
Boundary La. LA18 39 D3
Bowness Rd. LA18 39 C2
Butler St. LA18 39 C2
Buttermere Dri. LA18 39 C2
Cambridge St. LA18 39 C2
Castle St. LA18 39 D3
Church Wk. LA18 39 B2
Churchill Dri. LA18 39 D3
Cleator St. LA18 39 B2
Cook Rd. LA18 39 D3
Crown St. LA18 39 D3
Cumberland Clo. LA18 39 D3
Derwentwater Clo.
  LA18 39 C3
Devonshire Rd. LA18 39 D3
Earl St. LA18 39 D2
Egremont St. LA18 39 D3
Ennerdale Clo. LA18 39 C3
Fairfield Rd. LA18 39 C1
Festival Rd. LA18 39 C2

Finch St. LA18 39 C2
Furness St. LA18 39 E3
Grammerscroft. LA18 39 B3
Haverigg Rd. LA18 39 B4
Holborn Hill. LA18 39 B2
Hope St. LA18 39 E3
Horn Hill. LA18 39 C2
Huddleston Rd. LA18 39 C1
INDUSTRIAL & RETAIL:
  Devonshire Rd
  Ind Est. LA18 39 E3
*Jubilee Ct,
  Devonshire Rd. LA18 39 D3
Katharine St. LA18 39 D3
King St. LA18 39 D3
Kingsland Rd. LA18 39 C2
Lancashire Rd. LA18 39 C3
Langdale Clo. LA18 39 C3
Lapstone Rd. LA18 39 C2
Leyfield Clo. LA18 39 C2
Lincoln St. LA18 39 D3
Lonsdale Rd. LA18 39 D2
Lord St. LA18 39 C3
Lowther Rd. LA18 39 C3
Mainsgate Rd. LA18 39 D4
Market Sq. LA18 39 D2
Market St. LA18 39 D2
Millom Rd. LA18 39 D2
Moor Cotts. LA18 39 B3
Moor End. LA18 39 B4
Moor Pk. LA18 39 C3
Moor Rd. LA18 39 B3
Moor Ter. LA18 39 B3
Mountbatten Way.
  LA18 39 B2
Munroe Av. LA18 39 C1
Nelson St. LA18 39 D3
Newton St. LA18 39 D3
Newton Ter. LA18 39 B2
Nicholson Clo. LA18 39 C3
Old Moor Gdns. LA18 39 D3
Oxford St. LA18 39 D3
Palmers La. LA18 39 B2
Pannatt Hill. LA18 39 B2
Park Rd. LA18 39 C3
Peters Dri. LA18 39 B2
Queen St. LA18 39 D3
Queens Pk. LA18 39 B2
Richmond St. LA18 39 B2
Robinson Row. LA18 39 B2
Rottington Rd. LA18 39 D3
Rydal Clo. LA18 39 C3
St Georges Rd. LA18 39 C2
St Georges Ter. LA18 39 C2
Salthouse Rd. LA18 39 C2
Scales Vw. LA18 39 B2
Seathwaite Clo. LA18 39 C3
Settle St. LA18 39 C2
Station Rd. LA18 39 C2
Surrey St. LA18 39 D3
The Peel. LA18 39 E3
Thirlmere Clo. LA18 39 C3
Trinity Rd. LA18 39 C1
Victoria St. LA18 39 C2
Wasdale Rd. LA18 39 D3
Wellington St. LA18 39 D3
Whinlatter Clo. LA18 39 C3
Windermere Gdns.
  LA18 39 C3
Windsor St. LA18 39 D3

PENRITH

Albert St. CA11 41 B7
Alder Rd. CA11 40 F4
Alexandra Rd. CA11 40 B4
Anchor Clo. CA11 40 B2
Angel La. CA11 41 B7
Apple Tree Gdns. CA11 40 F4
*Arnisons Ct,
  Southend Rd. CA11 40 C4
Arthur St. CA11 41 B7
Ash Rd. CA11 40 E4
Askham Cres. CA11 40 D3
Aspen Gdns. CA11 40 F3
Auction Mart Rd. CA11 41 A8
Azalea Clo. CA11 40 F3
Balmoral Clo. CA11 40 B4
Barco Av. CA11 40 D4
Barton Vw. CA11 40 D3
Beacon Edge. CA11 40 C2
Beacon Pk. CA11 40 D2
Beacon Sq. CA11 40 D3
Beacon St. CA11 40 D2

Beatham Ct. CA11 40 B3
Beckside. CA11 40 F4
Beech Clo. CA11 40 F3
Beech Gdns. CA11 40 F3
Benson Row. CA11 40 D3
Berkeley Ct. CA11 40 A4
Birch Cres. CA11 40 F4
Blencathra Ct. CA11 41 C5
Bluebell La. CA11 41 A7
Bowerbank Way. CA11 40 A3
Brent Gdns. CA11 40 D3
Brent Rd. CA11 40 D3
Brentfield Ct. CA11 40 E3
Brentfield Way. CA11 40 D3
Bridge La. CA11 41 D5
Bridge St. CA11 40 B3
Brook St. CA11 41 B7
Brooklands Grange.
  CA11 40 E4
Brougham Av. CA10 41 F7
Brougham Hall Gdns.
  CA10 41 F7
Brougham St. CA11 40 B4
Brunswick Rd. CA11 41 A8
Brunswick Sq. CA11 41 A7
Brunswick Ter. CA11 41 A7
Burrowgate. CA11 41 B7
Canny Croft. CA11 40 C2
Carleton Av. CA10 40 F4
Carleton Derrick Dri.
  CA11 40 E3
Carleton Dri. CA11 40 D4
Carleton Fields. CA11 40 E3
Carleton Hall Gdns.
  CA10 41 E5
Carleton Hall Rd. CA10 41 E5
Carleton Hall Wk. CA10 41 E5
Carleton Hill Rd. CA11 40 F4
Carleton Mdws. CA11 40 E3
Carleton Pl. CA11 40 D4
Carleton Rd. CA11 40 D4
Castle Dri. CA11 41 B8
Castle Hill Rd. CA11 40 C4
Castle Ter. CA11 40 C4
Castlegate. CA11 41 A8
Castletown Ct. CA11 40 A3
Castletown Dri. CA11 40 A3
Cedar Clo. CA11 40 E4
Cherry Gdns. CA11 40 F4
Chestnut Clo. CA11 40 F4
Clifford Clo. CA11 41 C5
Clifford Ct. CA11 41 C5
Clifford Rd. CA11 41 B5
Cold Springs Pk. CA11 40 A4
Cookson Ct. CA11 40 A4
Corney Pl. CA11 40 B7
Corney Sq. CA11 40 C3
Corn Mkt. CA11 41 B8
Croft Av. CA11 40 C3
Croft Ter. CA11 40 C2
Cromwell Rd. CA11 41 A8
Cross La. CA11 40 B3
Cross St. CA11 40 B4
Crown Sq. CA11 41 B8
Crown Ter. CA11 40 D4
Cumberland Pl. CA11 40 E4
Cypress Way. CA11 40 F3
Devonshire Arc. CA11 41 B8
Devonshire St. CA11 41 B7
Dewhelpdale La. CA11 41 B7
Drovers La. CA11 40 B2
Drovers Mews. CA11 40 B2
Duke St. CA11 41 A7
Eamont Pk. CA10 41 E6
Eden Mount. CA11 41 A8
Elm Ct. CA11 41 A8
Elm Ter. CA11 41 A7
Exchange La. CA11 41 B8
Fairgate. CA11 40 D3
Fairhill Clo. CA11 40 C1
Fairhill Rd. CA11 40 B1
Fallowfield Ct. CA11 40 D3
Fell La. CA11 40 D3
Field House Gdns.
  CA11 40 C2
Folly La. CA11 40 A4
Foster St. CA11 40 B3
Frenchfield Gdns. CA11 40 F4
Frenchfield Way. CA11 40 F4
Friars Clo. CA11 40 D4
Friars Gro. CA11 40 D4
Friars Rise. CA11 40 D4
Friars Rd. CA11 40 D4
Friars Ter. CA11 40 D4
Garden Clo. CA11 41 A7
Gillan Way. CA11 41 B5

Gilwilly La. CA11 40 A3
Gilwilly Rd. CA11 40 A4
Glasson Ct. CA11 40 D4
Graham St. CA11 40 C3
Grahams La. CA11 41 B8
Great Dockray. CA11 41 B8
Green La. CA11 40 C1
Greystoke Clo. CA11 40 A4
Greystoke Pk Av. CA11 40 A4
Greystoke Pk Clo. CA11 40 A4
Greystoke Pk Rd. CA11 40 B4
Greystoke Rd. CA11 40 A4
Grove Ct. CA11 40 B3
Hallin Croft. CA11 40 D3
Hartness Rd. CA11 40 D3
Haweswater Clo. CA11 40 A4
Haweswater Rd. CA11 40 A4
Hawthorn Dri. CA11 40 F4
Helmsley Clo. CA11 40 F4
Helvelyn Ct. CA11 41 C5
Holly Clo. CA11 40 F3
Holme Riggs Av. CA11 41 C5
Horsley Ter. CA11 40 D2
Howard St. CA11 40 D3
Hunters La. CA11 41 B7
Huntley Av. CA11 41 C5
Huntley Ct. CA11 41 C5
Hutton Hill. CA11 40 D3
INDUSTRIAL & RETAIL:
  Penrith Ind Est. CA11 40 A4
  Skirsgill Business Pk.
  CA11 41 B6
Inglewood Rd. CA11 40 B1
Irving Ct. CA11 41 E5
James St. CA11 40 B3
Jasmine Clo. CA11 40 F3
Jubilee Clo. CA11 40 E4
Juniper Way. CA11 40 F3
King St. CA11 41 B8
Laburnum Way. CA11 40 F4
Lamley Gdns. CA11 40 C2
*Langton St,
  Southend Rd. CA11 40 C4
Larch Clo. CA11 40 F4
Lark La. CA11 40 B2
Little Dockray. CA11 41 B8
Lowther Glen. CA10 41 E7
Lowther St. CA11 40 C3
Macadam Way. CA11 40 B2
Macadams Gdns. CA11 40 C2
Maple Dri. CA11 40 E4
Mardale Av. CA11 40 A4
Mardale Rd. CA11 40 A4
Market Sq. CA11 41 B8
Mary Langley Way.
  CA11 41 E5
Mayburgh Av. CA11 41 C5
Mayburgh Clo. CA10 41 E7
Meadowcroft. CA11 40 E4
Meeting House La.
  CA11 41 B7
Middlegate. CA11 41 B7
Mile La. CA11 41 A6
Mill St. CA11 40 B3
Mill Ter. CA11 40 B4
Milner Mount. CA11 40 E3
Milton St. CA11 40 B2
Monks Clo. CA11 40 B2
Monnington Way. CA11 40 C2
Musgrave St. CA11 40 B4
Myers La. CA11 40 B4
Netherend Rd. CA11 41 C5
Neville Av. CA11 41 A8
Newlands Pl. CA11 40 A4
Newton Rd. CA11 40 A4
Nicholson La. CA11 40 D2
Norfolk Pl. CA11 40 B4
Norfolk Rd. CA11 40 B4
Oak Rd. CA11 40 E3
Old London Rd. CA11 40 D4
Park Clo. CA11 40 E4
Parkland Cres. CA11 40 E3
Parkland View. CA11 40 E3
Parklands Way. CA11 40 E4
Pategill Ct. CA11 40 D4
Pategill Pk. CA11 41 E5
Pategill Rd. CA11 40 D4
Pategill Wk. CA11 41 E5
Pear Tree Way. CA11 40 F3
Pearson Ct. CA11 40 D4
Pembroke Pl. CA11 40 C2
Pennine Way. CA11 40 D3
Penny Hill Pk. CA11 40 B2
Petteril Rd. CA11 40 B2
Poets La. CA11 41 A8
Porthouse Rd. CA11 41 A7

Portland Pl. CA11 41 A7
Prince Charles Clo. CA11 40 E4
Princes St. CA11 41 B8
Queen St. CA11 41 B7
Raiselands Croft. CA11 40 B2
Riggside. CA11 40 E4
Robinson St. CA11 40 B2
Roman Rd. CA11 40 D3
Roper St. CA11 40 D4
Rowcliffe La. CA11 41 B8
Rydal Ct. CA11 41 C5
Rydal Cres. CA11 41 C5
Salkeld Rd. CA11 40 B2
Sand Croft. CA11 40 D3
Sandgate. CA11 41 B7
Scaws Dri. CA11 40 D2
Scotland Rd. CA11 40 A1
Sim Ct. CA11 40 D4
Skirsgill Clo. CA11 41 B5
Skirsgill Gdns. CA11 41 B5
Skirsgill La. CA10 41 C6
Southend Rd. CA11 41 B8
Stalker Rd. CA11 40 A3
Stricklandgate. CA11 41 A7
Sycamore Dri. CA11 40 F4
Thacka La. CA11 40 A2
The Parklands. CA11 40 E3
Thirlmere Pk. CA11 41 C5
Tyne Clo Av. CA11 41 C5
Tyne Clo Ter. CA11 41 C5
Tynefield Ct. CA11 40 D4
Tynefield Dri. CA11 41 D5
Ullswater Rd. CA11 41 B5
Union La. CA11 40 B4
Victoria Rd. CA11 40 C4
Walker Rise. CA11 40 B2
Warwick Pl. CA11 41 A8
Watson Ter. CA11 41 A7
West La. CA11 41 A8
Wetheriggs La. CA11 41 C5
Wetheriggs Rise. CA11 41 C5
White Ox Way. CA11 40 B1
William St. CA11 41 B7
Willow Clo. CA11 40 E4
Windsor Ct. CA11 40 E4
Windsor Dri. CA11 40 B4
Wordsworth St. CA11 40 C3
York St. CA11 40 B3

SEASCALE

Albert St. CA20 42 A3
Coniston Av. CA20 42 B2
Crescent Cotts. CA20 42 A3
Crofthead Rd. CA20 42 B1
Cross Lanes. CA20 42 C1
Drigg Rd. CA20 42 A3
Eskdale Av. CA20 42 B2
Fell Vw Rd. CA20 42 C2
Gosforth Rd. CA20 42 A2
Green Clo. CA20 42 A2
Hallsenna La. CA20 42 C1
Hallsenna Rd. CA20 42 B2
Highfield Clo. CA20 42 C1
INDUSTRIAL & RETAIL:
Cross Lanes Business Centre. CA20 42 B1
Lingmell Cres. CA20 42 C2
Links Cres. CA20 42 A2
Railway Ter. CA20 42 A3
Santon Way. CA20 42 B2
Scawfell Cres. CA20 42 C2
Seascale Pk. CA20 42 C1
South Par. CA20 42 A3
The Banks. CA20 42 A2
The Crescent. CA20 42 A3
The Drive. CA20 42 C2
The Fairways. CA20 42 A2
Victoria Ter. CA20 42 A3
Wasdale Pk. CA20 42 A3
Wastwater Rise. CA20 42 C1
Whole House Rd. CA20 42 B2

SEDBERGH

Back La. LA10 42 C5
Bainbridge Rd. LA10 42 B5
Birks La. LA10 42 A6
Busk La. LA10 42 B5
Castlegarth. LA10 42 C5
Castlehaw. LA10 42 C5
Castlehaw La. LA10 42 C5
Cockle St. LA10 42 B5
Fairholme. LA10 42 B4
Fell Clo. LA10 42 C5
Finkle St. LA10 42 C5
Guldrey Fold. LA10 42 A5
Guldrey La. LA10 42 A5
Guldrey Ter. LA10 42 B5
Havera. LA10 42 B5
Highfield Rd. LA10 42 B5
Howgill La. LA10 42 A4
Joss La. LA10 42 C4
Loftus Hill. LA10 42 C5
Long La. LA10 42 C5
Low Langstaffe. LA10 42 C5
Main St. LA10 42 C5
Maryfell. LA10 42 C5
New St. LA10 42 C5
Queens Dri. LA10 42 A5
Rawthey Gdns. LA10 42 B5
Southfield Rd. LA10 42 A5
Station Rd. LA10 42 A5
Sycamore Av. LA10 42 B5
Thorns Bank. LA10 42 D5
Thorns La. LA10 42 D5
Vicarage La. LA10 42 C5
Winfield Rd. LA10 42 C4
Woodside Av. LA10 42 B5

SILLOTH

Barracks Bri. CA5 43 C2
Caldew St. CA5 43 B3
Church Ter. CA5 43 B3
Criffel St. CA5 43 B3
Eden St. CA5 43 B3
Esk St. CA5 43 B3
Fell Clo. CA5 43 C3
Fell Vw. CA5 43 C3
Holliday Cres. CA5 43 B4
INDUSTRIAL & RETAIL:
Station Rd Ind Est. CA5 43 B4
Latrigg St. CA5 43 B3
Lawn Ter. CA5 43 A3
Liddell St. CA5 43 B2
Links Clo. CA5 43 B4
Mary St. CA5 43 B3
Pennine Clo. CA5 43 C3
Pennine Vw. CA5 43 C3
Petteril St. CA5 43 B3
Petteril Ter. CA5 43 B3
School La. CA5 43 B2
Skiddaw Clo. CA5 43 C3
Skiddaw St. CA5 43 B3
Skinburness Cres. CA5 43 C1
Skinburness Dri. CA5 43 C1
Skinburness Rd. CA5 43 B2
Solway St. CA5 43 B3
Station Rd. CA5 43 B3
The Crofts. CA5 43 B4
Wampool St. CA5 43 B3
Waver St. CA5 43 B3
Wigton Rd. CA5 43 C3

STAVELEY

Back La. LA8 48 C4
Beck Nook. LA8 48 B5
Brow La. LA8 48 B4
Burneside Rd. LA8 48 C4
Crag Vw. LA8 48 C4
Crook Rd. LA8 48 B6
Danes Cres. LA8 48 B5
Fairfield Clo. LA8 48 C5
Gowan Clo. LA8 48 B5
Gowan Cres. LA8 48 C5
Gowan Ter. LA8 48 C5
Hall La. LA8 48 C4
Kendal Rd. LA8 48 C5
Kent Dri. LA8 48 C4
Kentmere Rd. LA8 48 C4
Main St. LA8 48 C5
Raven Garth. LA8 48 B4
Rawes Garth. LA8 48 B5
School La. LA8 48 B4
Scroggs Clo. LA8 48 C4
Seed Howe. LA8 48 A4
Seedfield. LA8 48 C5
Station La. LA8 48 C5
Station Rd. LA8 48 C5
*Station Yd, Station La. LA8 48 C5
The Banks. LA8 48 C5
Windermere Rd. LA8 48 A4

ULVERSTON

Acacia Rd. LA12 45 E5
Ainslie St. LA12 45 E2
Ainsworth St. LA12 45 E2
Aldwych Ter. LA12 45 E3
Alexander Rd. LA12 45 E3
Almond Rd. LA12 45 E5
Appletree Rd. LA12 45 E5
Argyle St. LA12 45 E3
Ash Gro. LA12 45 E5
Back Ford Rd. LA12 45 E2
Back La. LA12 45 E2
Back Sun St. LA12 44 D2
Bailey St. LA12 45 F2
Bay Tree Rd. LA12 45 F5
Beckside Rd. LA12 44 D1
Beech Bank. LA12 45 E2
Beech Dri. LA12 45 E4
Beechlands. LA12 45 E4
Belmont. LA12 45 E1
*Benson St, Queen St. LA12 45 E3
Bigland Dri. LA12 45 E6
Birchwood Clo. LA12 45 E6
Birchwood Dri. LA12 45 E6
Birkett Dri. LA12 44 D6
Birkrigg Clo. LA12 44 B6
Boarbank Rd. LA12 45 E6
Bracken Gro. LA12 44 B5
Braddyll Ter. LA12 45 E3
Brewery St. LA12 45 E2
Brick Kiln Rd. LA12 45 F5
Brogden St. LA12 45 E2
Brookvale. LA12 44 B5
Burlington St. LA12 45 E2
Byron St. LA12 45 F2
Campfield Rd. LA12 45 E6
Canal Sq. LA12 45 G3
Canal St. LA12 45 F2
Caraway Clo. LA12 44 D5
Carlton Dri. LA12 44 D6
Cartmel Dri. LA12 45 E6
Casson St. LA12 45 E2
Cavendish St. LA12 45 E3
Central Dri. LA12 45 E5
Chapel St. LA12 45 E3
Cherry Tree Av. LA12 45 E4
Chestnut Gro. LA12 45 E4
Chittery La. LA12 45 E1
Church Fields. LA12 45 E1
Church Wk. LA12 45 E2
Clarence St. LA12 45 E2
Colthouse La. LA12 44 D6
Conishead Rd. LA12 45 E3
County Rd. LA12 45 E3
Cox St. LA12 45 E3
Cross La. LA12 45 H4
Cross A Moor. LA12 44 A5
Crosslands Clo. LA12 44 B5
Dale St. LA12 45 F2
Daltongate. LA12 44 D3
Daltongate Ct. LA12 44 D2
Derwent Pl. LA12 45 F4
Devonshire Rd. LA12 45 F2
Dorchester Cres. LA12 44 D6
Eden Mt. LA12 45 E6
*Edmonson St, Tower St. LA12 45 F2
Ellerside. LA12 45 E3
Fallowfield Av. LA12 44 D3
Fell St. LA12 45 F2
Fell Vw. LA12 44 B5
Flan Clo. LA12 45 E1
Ford Pk Cres. LA12 45 F2
Fountain St. LA12 45 E2
Fox St. LA12 44 B5
Garden Lea. LA12 45 E3
Garden Ter. LA12 44 D1
Goad St. LA12 44 B4
Grasmere Rd. LA12 45 F3
Green Bank. LA12 45 E2
Hallfield. LA12 44 D5
Hampsfell Rd. LA12 45 E6
Hart St. LA12 45 E2
Hartley St. LA12 45 E3
Hawthorn Av. LA12 45 E5
Hazelcroft Gdns. LA12 44 D3
Hazeltree Rd. LA12 45 E5
Heather Bank. LA12 44 B5
Hest Vw Rd. LA12 45 E6
Heversham Clo. LA12 45 E5
Hill Fall. LA12 45 F3
Hillside Rd. LA12 45 E5
Hoad La. LA12 45 F1
Holly Bank. LA12 45 E5
INDUSTRIAL & RETAIL:
Lightburn Trading Est. LA12 44 D3
South Ulverston Ind Area.LA12 45 H3
Jefferson Dri. LA12 44 D6
Kennedy St. LA12 45 H3
King St. LA12 45 E2
Kings Rd. LA12 45 E3
Kingsley Av. LA12 44 B4
Kingsway. LA12 45 F2
Leather La. LA12 44 D2
Lightburn Av. LA12 45 E3
Lightburn Rd. LA12 44 D3
Lime Tree Rd. LA12 45 E4
Lower Brook St. LA12 45 E2
Lund Rd. LA12 45 F3
Lund Ter. LA12 45 F3
Lyndhurst Pk. LA12 44 D4
Machell Clo. LA12 44 D3
Main Rd. LA12 44 B6
Maple Av. LA12 45 E5
Market St. LA12 45 E2
Mayfield Rd. LA12 44 D3
Meadowside. LA12 44 B5
Mearness Dri. LA12 45 E6
Meeting House La. LA12 44 D5
Mill St. LA12 45 E2
Moorgarth. LA12 44 B5
Morecambe Rd. LA12 45 F3
Mt Barnard Vw. LA12 45 E5
Mountbarrow Rd. LA12 44 D6
Mowings La. LA12 44 D1
Neville St. LA12 45 E3
New Church La. LA12 44 D3
New Market St. LA12 45 E2
Newland Rd. LA12 45 F2
Newton St. LA12 45 E2
Next Ness La. LA12 45 G2
North Lonsdale Rd. LA12 45 G2
North Lonsdale Ter. LA12 45 F2
Oakwood Dri. LA12 45 E5
Old Hall Dri. LA12 44 D1
Old Hall Rd. LA12 44 D1
Outcast. LA12 45 G4
Oxford St. LA12 45 E3
Park Av. LA12 44 B5
Park Dri. LA12 45 E4
Park Field. LA12 44 B6
Park Rd. LA12 44 B4
Park Side. LA12 44 B5
Parkhead Rd. LA12 45 E6
Pennington La. LA12 44 C3
Pine Tree Rd. LA12 45 E5
Poplar Gro. LA12 45 F2
Princes St. LA12 45 E3
Priory Ct. LA12 45 F4
Priory Rd. LA12 45 F4
Quaker Fold. LA12 44 D5
Quay St. LA12 45 F2
Quebec St. LA12 45 F3
Queen St. LA12 45 E3
Rake Head Clo. LA12 44 D5
Rake La. LA12 45 E5
Rowan Av. LA12 45 E5
Rufus La. LA12 44 B4
Rusland Cres. LA12 44 D6
Rydal Rd. LA12 45 F3
St Davids Rd. LA12 45 E2
Sands Clo. LA12 45 E6
Sands Rd. LA12 45 E6
Savoy Gdns. LA12 44 D6
Sea Vw. LA12 45 E2
Sog La. LA12 44 A5
Soutergate. LA12 45 E2
Spout La. LA12 45 E2
Spring Vale. LA12 44 B6
Springfield Av. LA12 45 E4
Springfield Pk Rd. LA12 44 D4
Springfield Rd. LA12 45 E5
Stanley St. LA12 45 E2
Star St. LA12 44 D2
Steel St. LA12 45 G3
Stockbridge La. LA12 44 C2
Stonecross Gdns. LA12 44 D2
Stony Dale. LA12 45 E6
Sun St. LA12 44 D2
Sunderland Ter. LA12 45 F2
Swan St. LA12 45 F2
Swarthdale Av. LA12 45 E5
Swarthmoor Hall La. LA12 44 C5
Sycamore Av. LA12 45 E4
Tarn Clo. LA12 44 C2
Tarnside. LA12 45 E2
Tebay La. LA12 45 G1
The Crest. LA12 44 D4
The Drive. LA12 44 D4
The Ellers. LA12 45 E3
The Gill. LA12 44 D2
The Laurels. LA12 44 B5
Theatre St. LA12 45 E3
Tower St. LA12 45 F2
Town Bank Rd. LA12 45 E1
Town Bank Ter. LA12 45 E1
Town St. LA12 45 E2
Town Vw Rd. LA12 45 E1
Trinity Gdns. LA12 44 D3
Trinkeld Av. LA12 44 B6
Ullswater Clo. LA12 45 F3
Ulverston Rd. LA12 44 A6
Underwood Rd. LA12 45 E5
Union La. LA12 44 D2
Union St. LA12 45 E2
Upper Brook St. LA12 44 D2
Urswick Rd. LA12 44 C6
Victoria Rd. LA12 45 E3
Watery La. LA12 45 F3
Well Head. LA12 45 E2
Well La. LA12 45 F3
West End La. LA12 45 F5
West Hills Dri. LA12 44 D6
Weston Av. LA12 44 D5
Whinfield Rd. LA12 45 E1
William St. LA12 45 F2
Willow Ct. LA12 44 B5
Willow Dene Gdns. LA12 44 D1
Windsor Cres. LA12 44 D6
Woodland Rd. LA12 44 D3
Yealand Dri. LA12 45 E5
Yewbarrow Rd. LA12 45 E6

WETHERAL

Clints Rd. CA4 48 D2
Croft Pk. CA4 48 B2
Elm Garth. CA4 48 A1
Faustin Hill. CA4 48 B1
Geltsdale Gdns. CA4 48 B1
Goosegarth. CA4 48 A2
Greenacres. CA4 48 A1
Hallmoor Ct. CA4 48 B2
Jennet Croft. CA4 48 B2
Plains Rd. CA4 48 A1
Sandy La. CA4 48 D2
Steeles Bank. CA4 48 B1
The Beeches. CA4 48 C2
The Glebe. CA4 48 B3
The Green. CA4 48 B2
The Orchard. CA4 48 C3
Wheatsheaf Gdns. CA4 48 B3
Whitegate. CA4 48 B2
Woodlands. CA4 48 C2

WHITEHAVEN

Acer Gro. CA28 46 D3
Albion St. CA28 46 B1
Arrowthwaite. CA28 46 B2
Ashleigh Pl. CA28 46 D2
Ashness Clo. CA28 46 C6
Back Corkickle. CA28 46 C1
Balmoral Rd. CA28 47 E2
Basket Rd. CA28 46 A1
Beckside. CA28 47 E3
Bedford St. CA28 47 E3
Bleng Av. CA28 46 D2
Borrowdale Rd. CA28 46 C6
Bowfell Rd. CA28 46 D6
Bowness Rd. CA28 46 C5
Brakeside Gdns. CA28 46 B4
Burnmoor Av. CA28 46 C4
Buttermere Av. CA28 46 A4
Caldbeck Rd. CA28 47 E1
Calder Av. CA28 46 C2
Cambridge Rd. CA28 47 E4
Carlton Dri. CA28 47 E2

WORKINGTON

ESTATE PUBLICATIONS

RED BOOKS

ALDERSHOT, CAMBERLEY
ALFRETON, BELPER, RIPLEY
ASHFORD, TENTERDEN
AYLESBURY, TRING
BANGOR, CAERNARFON
BARNSTAPLE, BIDEFORD
BASILDON, BILLERICAY
BASINGSTOKE, ANDOVER
BATH, BRADFORD-ON-AVON
BEDFORD
BIRMINGHAM, WOLVERHAMPTON, COVENTRY
BODMIN, WADEBRIDGE
BOURNEMOUTH, POOLE, CHRISTCHURCH
BRACKNELL
BRENTWOOD
BRIGHTON, LEWES, NEWHAVEN, SEAFORD
BRISTOL
BROMLEY (London Borough)
BURTON-UPON-TRENT, SWADLINCOTE
BURY ST. EDMUNDS
CAMBRIDGE
CARDIFF
CARLISLE
CHELMSFORD, BRAINTREE, MALDON, WITHAM
CHESTER
CHESTERFIELD
CHICHESTER, BOGNOR REGIS
CHIPPENHAM, CALNE
COLCHESTER, CLACTON
CORBY, KETTERING
COVENTRY
CRAWLEY & MID SUSSEX
CREWE
DERBY, HEANOR, CASTLE DONINGTON
EASTBOURNE, BEXHILL, SEAFORD, NEWHAVEN
EDINBURGH, MUSSELBURGH, PENICUIK
EXETER, EXMOUTH
FALKIRK, GRANGEMOUTH
FAREHAM, GOSPORT
FLINTSHIRE TOWNS
FOLKESTONE, DOVER, DEAL & ROMNEY MARSH
GLASGOW, & PAISLEY
GLOUCESTER, CHELTENHAM
GRAVESEND, DARTFORD
GRAYS, THURROCK
GREAT YARMOUTH, LOWESTOFT
GRIMSBY, CLEETHORPES
GUILDFORD, WOKING
HARLOW, BISHOPS STORTFORD
HARROGATE, KNARESBOROUGH
HASTINGS, BEXHILL, RYE
HEREFORD
HERTFORD, HODDESDON, WARE
HIGH WYCOMBE
HUNTINGDON, ST. NEOTS
IPSWICH, FELIXSTOWE
ISLE OF MAN
ISLE OF WIGHT TOWNS
KENDAL, WINDERMERE
KIDDERMINSTER
KINGSTON-UPON-HULL
LANCASTER, MORECAMBE
LEICESTER, LOUGHBOROUGH
LINCOLN
LLANDUDNO, COLWYN BAY
LUTON, DUNSTABLE
MACCLESFIELD
MAIDSTONE
MANSFIELD, MANSFIELD WOODHOUSE
MEDWAY, GILLINGHAM
MILTON KEYNES
NEW FOREST TOWNS
NEWBURY, THATCHAM
NEWPORT, CHEPSTOW
NEWQUAY
NEWTOWN, WELSHPOOL
NORTHAMPTON
NORTHWICH, WINSFORD
NORWICH
NOTTINGHAM, EASTWOOD, HUCKNALL, ILKESTON
NUNEATON, BEDWORTH
OXFORD, ABINGDON
PENZANCE, ST. IVES
PERTH
PETERBOROUGH
PLYMOUTH, IVYBRIDGE, SALTASH, TORPOINT
PORTSMOUTH, HAVANT, WATERLOOVILLE
READING
REDDITCH, BROMSGROVE

REIGATE, BANSTEAD, LEATHERHEAD, DORKING
RHYL, PRESTATYN
RUGBY
ST. ALBANS, WELWYN, HATFIELD
ST. AUSTELL
SALISBURY, AMESBURY, WILTON
SCUNTHORPE
SEVENOAKS
SHREWSBURY
SITTINGBOURNE, FAVERSHAM, ISLE OF SHEPPEY
SLOUGH, MAIDENHEAD, WINDSOR
SOUTHAMPTON, EASTLEIGH
SOUTHEND-ON-SEA
STAFFORD
STEVENAGE, HITCHIN, LETCHWORTH
STIRLING
STOKE-ON-TRENT
STROUD, NAILSWORTH
SWANSEA, NEATH, PORT TALBOT
SWINDON, CHIPPENHAM, MARLBOROUGH
TAUNTON, BRIDGWATER
TELFORD
THANET, CANTERBURY, HERNE BAY, WHITSTABLE
TORBAY (Torquay, Paignton, Newton Abbot)
TROWBRIDGE, FROME
TRURO, FALMOUTH
TUNBRIDGE WELLS, TONBRIDGE, CROWBOROUGH
WARWICK, ROYAL LEAMINGTON SPA &
   STRATFORD UPON AVON
WATFORD, HEMEL HEMPSTEAD
WELLINGBOROUGH
WELLS, GLASTONBURY
WESTON-SUPER-MARE, CLEVEDON
WEYMOUTH, DORCHESTER
WINCHESTER, NEW ARLESFORD
WORCESTER, DROITWICH
WORKINGTON, WHITEHAVEN
WORTHING, LITTLEHAMPTON, ARUNDEL
WREXHAM
YORK

COUNTY RED BOOKS (Town Centre Maps)

BEDFORDSHIRE
BERKSHIRE
BUCKINGHAMSHIRE
CAMBRIDGESHIRE
CHESHIRE
CORNWALL
DERBYSHIRE
DEVON
DORSET
ESSEX
GLOUCESTERSHIRE
HAMPSHIRE
HEREFORDSHIRE
HERTFORDSHIRE
KENT
LEICESTERSHIRE & RUTLAND
LINCOLNSHIRE
NORFOLK
NORTHAMPTONSHIRE
NOTTINGHAMSHIRE
OXFORDSHIRE
SHROPSHIRE
SOMERSET
STAFFORDSHIRE
SUFFOLK
SURREY
SUSSEX (EAST)
SUSSEX (WEST)
WILTSHIRE
WORCESTERSHIRE

OTHER MAPS

KENT TO CORNWALL (1:460,000)
CHINA (1:6,000,000)
INDIA (1:3,750,000)
INDONESIA (1:4,000,000)
NEPAL (1,800,000)
SOUTH EAST ASIA (1:6,000,000)
THAILAND (1:1,600,000)

STREET PLANS

CARDIFF
EDINBURGH TOURIST PLAN
ST. ALBANS
WOLVERHAMPTON

OFFICIAL TOURIST & LEISURE MAPS

SOUTH EAST ENGLAND (1:200,000)
KENT & EAST SUSSEX (1:150,000)
SUSSEX & SURREY (1:150,000)
SUSSEX (1:50,000)
SOUTHERN ENGLAND (1:200,000)
ISLE OF WIGHT (1:50,000)
WESSEX (1:200,000)
DORSET (1:150,000)
DEVON & CORNWALL (1:200,000)
CORNWALL (1:180,000)
DEVON (1:200,000)
DARTMOOR & SOUTH DEVON COAST (1:100,000)
EXMOOR & NORTH DEVON COAST (1:100,000)
GREATER LONDON M25 (1:80,000)
EAST ANGLIA (1:200,000)
CHILTERNS & THAMES VALLEY (1:200,000)
THE COTSWOLDS (1:110,000)
COTSWOLDS & SEVERN VALLEY (1:200,000)
WALES (1:250,000)
THE SHIRES OF MIDDLE ENGLAND (1:250,000)
THE MID SHIRES (Staffs, Shrops, etc.) (1:200,000)
PEAK DISTRICT (1:100,000)
SNOWDONIA (1:125,000)
YORKSHIRE (1:200,000)
YORKSHIRE DALES (1:125,000)
NORTH YORKSHIRE MOORS (1:125,000)
NORTH WEST ENGLAND (1:200,000)
ISLE OF MAN (1:60,000)
NORTH PENNINES & LAKES (1:200,000)
LAKE DISTRICT (1:75,000)
BORDERS OF ENGLAND & SCOTLAND (1:200,000)
BURNS COUNTRY (1:200,000)
HEART OF SCOTLAND (1:200,000)
GREATER GLASGOW (1:150,000)
EDINBURGH & THE LOTHIANS (1:150,000)
ISLE OF ARRAN (1:63,360)
FIFE (1:100,000)
LOCH LOMOND & TROSSACHS (1:150,000)
ARGYLL THE ISLES & LOCH LOMOND (1:275,000)
PERTHSHIRE, DUNDEE & ANGUS (1:150,000)
FORT WILLIAM, BEN NEVIS, GLEN COE (1:185,000)
IONA (1:10,000) & MULL (1:115,000)
GRAMPIAN HIGHLANDS (1:185,000)
LOCH NESS & INVERNESS (1:150,000)
SKYE & LOCHALSH (1:130,000)
ARGYLL & THE ISLES (1:200,000)
CAITHNESS & SUTHERLAND (1:185,000)
HIGHLANDS OF SCOTLAND (1:275,000)
WESTERN ISLES (1:125,000)
ORKNEY & SHETLAND (1:128,000)
ENGLAND & WALES (1:650,000)
SCOTLAND (1:500,000)
HISTORIC SCOTLAND (1:500,000)
SCOTLAND CLAN MAP (1:625,000)
BRITISH ISLES (1:1,100,000)
GREAT BRITAIN (1:1,100,000)

EUROPEAN LEISURE MAPS

EUROPE (1:3,100,000)
BENELUX (1:600,000)
FRANCE (1:1,000,000)
GERMANY (1:750,000)
IRELAND (1:625,000)
ITALY (1:1,000,000)
SPAIN & PORTUGAL (1:1,000,000)
CROSS CHANNEL VISITORS' MAP (1:700,000)
WORLD (1:29,000,000)
WORLD FLAT

TOWNS IN NORTHERN FRANCE STREET ATLAS
BOULOGNE SHOPPERS MAP
CALAIS SHOPPERS MAP
DIEPPE SHOPPERS MAP

ESTATE PUBLICATIONS are also
Distributors in the UK for:

HALLWAG, Switzerland
HEMA, Australia
INTERNATIONAL TRAVEL MAPS, Canada
ORDNANCE SURVEY

Catalogue and prices from:
ESTATE PUBLICATIONS
Bridewell House, Tenterden, Kent. TN30 6EP.
Tel: 01580 764225   Fax: 01580 763720
www.estate-publications.co.uk